By George

A Collection of Childhood Experiences
And
Other Anecdotes

By George Herbert Stansbury Jr.
1893 - 1979

Selected & Edited
By James A. Stansbury and Paul S. Stansbury

Sheppard Press

Sheppard Press
461 Boone Trail
Danville, Kentucky 40422

Printed in the United States of America
ISBN 978-0-9986516-2-0 paperback

Cover Graphics by Paul Stansbury

Contents

INTRODUCTION

George Herbert Stansbury Senior left his home in Newark, New Jersey in the early 1880's to seek his fortune in Franklin, Pennsylvania, taking employment with the Eclipse Refinery. This was the time of the emerging oil boom and thousands flocked to Western Pennsylvania to seek their fortunes. Eclipse was later to be purchased by John D. Rockefeller's Standard Oil Company.

After establishing himself, George returned to New York in 1884 to marry his sweetheart, Alice Lincoln Hatcher. Together, they returned to Franklin, where they established their home at 12 Sixteenth Street. They joined St. John's Episcopal Church. While residing in Franklin, three sons were born. Paul Wood Stansbury (most often referred to by the family as P.W.) was born in 1886, Charles Bertram Stansbury (Bert as he was known) was born in 1891, and George Herbert Stansbury Jr. (called by many names, Jack being the most common) was born in 1893.

In 1903, following his career with Standard Oil, George Herbert Stansbury Sr. moved the family to Cincinnati, Ohio. The family established their home at 321 McGregor Street. They were there but a few years before the family finally moved to Louisville, Kentucky, where they were to remain, establishing their home at 52 Castlewood Place. By the time they moved to Louisville, George Herbert Stansbury Sr. was a vice president of the Standard Oil Company.

During a ten year period from 1964 through 1974, George Herbert Stansbury Jr., then retired from the Standard Oil Company, sat at his typewriter and composed reminiscences of his childhood as well as letters and other musings which he sent primarily to his brother

P.W. After George's death in 1979, his wife of 60 years, Frances Fawcett Stansbury, passed them along to their oldest grandchild, James Andrew Stansbury. In 1991, James compiled the materials, which he entitled *By George*, and commissioned hard bound copies which he gave to family members as Christmas presents.

This collection covers the period during which George Herbert Stansbury Jr. lived in Franklin, Pennsylvania and Cincinnati, Ohio. His earliest reminiscence is from 1897 when he was four years old.

We are certain the experiences and anecdotes, which he calls "And then there was the time" items, were written as part of his ongoing dialogue with his brother P.W. These were almost always separate documents accompanying the letters he sent to his brothers. Whether his brother Bert received copies is unknown.

Also included are excerpts from some of the letters themselves George Herbert Stansbury Jr. wrote. All excerpts, save one to Bert, are from letters to P.W. Some refer to his "And then there was the time" items, and some contain additional commentary on his early childhood.

A special thanks goes out to the Venango County Historical Society and the staff of St. John's Episcopal Church in Franklin, Pennsylvania for their gracious assistance in the research of this collection.

These experiences and anecdotes, are presented as they were originally written, with as little editorial interference as possible. The footnotes have been added to provide useful information. Only the most obvious and readily recognizable typographic errors have been corrected. Vernacular and syntax have been preserved. After all, these were not created as a literary work. Rather, they are fond reminiscences shared between brothers. As such, they deserve to be presented in their original form.

FRANKLIN, PENNSYLVANIA

THE GOLDILOCKS SLEIGH
(Circa 1897)

And then there was the time (to be exact, it was the day after Christmas) when I was four years old. My father had purchased, for me, a sled which I didn't like. I was a little stinker. I told my mother about the things I did not like about the sled and she suggested that I take it back to the store and either have my money refunded or trade it in for one that suited me. I had, in fact, seen this sled in Rollya's[1] window a few days before, which was exactly to my liking. Its price was one dollar, Riva Rollya had told me so.

My mother, who was alert to all of the family's financial transactions, told me that the Christmas sled cost sixty-five cents, and to make matters more complex, it had not been bought, by my father, from Rollya's store. But there was a way out - my mother suggested that I asked my father for a loan of thirty-five cents (She was phenomenal at the arithmetic), take the sled back and demand a complete refund, unless, of course, I could get a suitable one dollar sled in that store.

The store was on the far side of Thirteenth Street somewhere around Elk. This made the matter of returning it rather complicated, for even if the name of the store had been supplied, I wouldn't be able to find it because I couldn't yet read. Also, I was a little bit concerned about my ability to demand a cash refund or to count the money if it was forthcoming.

Again my mother rescued me from a dilemma. She simply asked George Allen, who was visiting with my father that afternoon, if he would accompany me on my mission. The thirty-five cent loan from my father was easily procured, apparently mother had tipped him off about my dissatisfaction with the sled. But I've told you that I was a little stinker. You know, looking a gift sled in the mouth, and all that jazz.

---

[1] Most likely Rallya & Griffin Stationer and Bookstore.

George readily agreed to go with me to return the sled but he wanted to know what was wrong with it. I assured him that there was nothing broken on the sled - it just didn't suit me - somewhat like a fairytale sleigh on which the blonde princess was want to ride. It had curlicues at the front and besides it wrote too high for "belly-bustering."

We, George and I, carried the sled down the front steps and my mother cautioned me that I was not to drag it or I might have difficulty making the store man believe it was new. So George picked it up by the curlicues of one runner and carried it as we walked down Liberty Street.

Colonel Lewis was standing on his 'snow-cleared' sidewalk as George and I came by. He greeted us with, "a Merry Christmas boys."

George return this salutation in kind and I doffed my cap to him and murmured "Christmas," at the same time cringing bashfully behind George. The Colonel reached into his pocket and held out a quarter toward me recommending that I accept it. More bashfulness on my part and more cringing as I muttered, "No thanks, I can't," but on specific urging from George, I finally accepted the quarter, with again a muttered, "Oh well."

We continued down Liberty to Thirteenth and as we walked George assured me that the Colonel could well afford the quarter and that by accepting it, the Colonel would not have to cut down his customary breakfast of two eggs to one on the morrow.

George made the negotiations in the store while I looked over the stock of sleds for a more suitable one for a handsome, robust, daring and "devil-may-care" boy like myself. I had figured that I could go as high as a dollar.

Then I remembered the extra quarter that was in my pants pocket and discovered a "Ball Bearing Bobsled" which George told me cost a dollar and a quarter, the exact amount that I now was entitled to spend. We bought this miniature bobsled and George, because we had no rope to pull with, took it under his arm and we hurried home.

That cap tipping incident was completely voluntary on my part. In fact it wasn't until about two years later, when Bert and I were

4

strolling along Thirteenth Street, when I was told (by Bert) that it was neither customary nor essential that I doffed my cap to a gentleman. We had met Mr. Steinbrenner in the vicinity of Woodburn, Cone and Steele's massive dry goods store and I dutifully doffed my cap to him as we passed. "Oh Jim, you shouldn't tip your hat to him, he's a man!" I was embarrassed by the lack of decorum which I had exhibited. But remembering that Mr. Steinbrenner was responsible for our black dog Joe having been given to us, I tried to defend my stupidity by reminding my brother of this fact. He replied, "That doesn't make any difference he's a man!" From that day on I have never tip my hat to anyone who wasn't wearing a skirt.

Oh, but I was telling you about that little bobsled wasn't I. We got home and found a nice piece of close line with which to steer it. After a dozen or more attempts to slide on it - the front runners turn to easily and it was so low that the snow always seem to pile up in my face. I decided to abandon it and stood it up in the barn, leaning against the bran bin. Next day my mother told me that I must put it somewhere else as it interfered with the hinged cover on the bin. Not wishing to further display my folly of purchasing it, I, with some difficulty, carted it up the vertical ladder to the hayloft where it served admirably as a bench on which to sit while cracking butternuts at the outside of the loft door.

And so that miniature bobsled may still be up there by the door provided of course, that the little red barn is still standing. - So what?

OH GEORGE, WILL YOU NEVER LEARN?
(Circa 1897)

And then there was the time when I had just received my weekly stipend, allowance, or gratuity: a bright new 1897 nickel which, judging from it's silvery sheen, had never once been spent. It was truly a treasure, and as I had nothing in mind at the moment which I particularly craved, decided to emulate Captain Kidd and bury it.

After careful consideration, I chose the most unlikely spot in the immediate vicinity to conceal my wealth: the terrace directly outside of our dining room window. With great care and the hatchet from the junk drawer, about a six inch square of sod was removed from the proposed spot, a couple more digs with the hatchet and the nickel was concealed in a nest of soft brown loam. I tamped down the earth, replaced the divot and turned to find a suitable marker. At that very instant, I got a flash of Eddie's head disappearing behind the window sill of the Riesenman's pantry window.

Gadzooks! I had been spied upon.

Eddie was a strange combination of pleasing playmate and sneaky snooper. And he had an unfortunate penchant for lying when the truth would be far simpler and would serve to promote his own devices far more readily than a lie. As an example – that day when Bert had about completed his latest creation - a back yard refrigerator, which he designed, from all things, an old open slatted orange crate. He had stood the crate on end and bashed out the top partition so that the ice, a chunk of which could stealthily be procured from the, one-man ice wagon while the ice man was in a neighbors kitchen making a delivery. The open slat-work sides would allow the sun and hot summer air easy access to the ice and vegetables. But, as Bert explained it, his refrigerator was to be placed in a shady spot near the house and the openings between the slats would allow the water from the melting ice to drain more freely. And in addition, the "pure, clean, fresh summer air would circulate through the lower compartment where the fruits and

6

vegetables were stored and tend to preserve their freshness." - A credible explanation, but even at the age of four, I couldn't quite understand how the produce in the bottom compartment would even suspect that there was ice in the upper compartment, much less, that it was there to keep them fresh and cool.

While brother Bert was completing the leather hinged door to the lower level, or goodies department, of the crate, he suggested that Eddie and I forage for rations. We sneaked into the Donald McCalmont truck garden and shortly emerged with two tomatoes and an enormous cucumber. Eddie was so proud of this colossal vegetable that he shouted hilariously when he found it and we both had to duck quickly behind the foliage to keep from being discovered by Douglas the negro utility man, who at this juncture, was fortunately asleep on the back steps of the McCalmont house.

Eddie bore the cucumber triumphantly back to the refrigeration department, his mother appeared in an upstairs window of Eddie's home and Eddie hurriedly, but ineffectively, attempted to conceal his prize behind his back. "Edward," called his mother, "what have you got there?"

"Nothing" replied Eddie.

"Hold it up and let me see," called mother. Eddie dropped the cucumber behind his back and held up his, now empty, hands for inspection. Oh the treachery of it all! The cucumber landed on its end, rebounded like a rubber ball, or a taut bow, and came to rest directly at his feet, but now in front of him and in full view of his mother. "Edward come in this house immediately." shouted Mrs. Riesenman.

"We'll keep it cool for you," whispered Bert, as Eddie trod his forlorn way into the house for proper punishment.

If he had admitted the obvious, that he had swiped a cucumber, he probably would not have been spanked, but his denial assured it.

But back to the treasure, I carefully dug up the nickel, which had lost but little of it's luster from the short encounter with the moist earth, but after wiping it clean I decided that it should be wrapped in some sort of a protective covering before being concealed again. I found an

7

outside envelope from a long since used package of Beemans Pepsin Gum, carefully enclosed the nickel in it and using a stray bit of red crayon, I marked an 'X' on the stern face of Mr. Beeman, thus putting my personal seal of ownership on the treasure, according to the best pirate practices. Then, selecting a spot on the terrace approximately thirty feet nearer the street, and out of the line of sight from Eddie's pantry window, I again buried the nickel, this time marking the hiding place with an old, discarded, one-legged clothes pin.

After supper, my concern for the safety of the cache prompted a hasty return to the terrace and a search for the amputeed clothes pin. Lo and behold, the pin was there alright but it was standing on it's head, it's single leg, by some odd circumstance, was pointing incriminatingly towards the Riesenman house. Puzzled and somewhat disturbed by this turn of events, I dug furiously and sifted the dirt carefully through my fingers, but no trace of that errant nickel could be found. I dug deeper and deeper without success and finally in a frenzy of despair, sought out the original hiding place, diligently dug and dug, sifted and sifted, but without even finding a trace of the nickel or the wrapper.

Eddie soon joined me, stood with his hands in his pants pockets and casually inquired, "What ya doin?" A flash of genius hit me. If I told Eddie the true purpose of my activity, he might well volunteer to help in the search and that would cut down by half the chances of my ever recovering the nickel. So I made up the impossible excuse that I was just cleaning the rust off the hatchet blade by digging in the terrace. "Oh sure," sez Eddie and retreated to his back porch.

I sought sanctuary in the kitchen and when Eddie went back into his house, resumed my scrupulous search, concentrating on the second place of concealment, removed all of the loose dirt and sifted it diligently again and again, the nickel was not there. I finally retired, defeated.

The following morning after a hurried breakfast, I walked out on the front porch to consider again the possibility that my search had not been thorough enough on the preceding day. The bakery wagon had just passed by with the usual clanging of the hand bell. Eddie was crouched on the curb in front of his house stuffing his mouth with what remained of a chocolate cocoanut cream patty - one of those delightful confections carried by the bakery man and sold from the wagon at five cents apiece. Eddie waved at me, mumbled something about his mother calling him and disappeared into the house. Even with such convincing evidence, my ever alert mind had no thought of incriminating Eddie and I got the hatchet out again and walked to the terrace, determined to find my buried nickel. On approaching the driveway, I noticed a piece of bakery paper, smeared with chocolate, in the gutter where Eddie had been sitting. On closer inspection, I also found a Beemans gum wrapper with a smeared red X obliterating the countenance of the manufacturer. Finally I had seen the light. How gullible can a small boy get?

MUD MELANGE
(Circa 1898)

And then there was the time when Bobby Read and I found a number of large leaved, strange looking plants in Mr. Barnes' front yard. At my suggestion we pulled one up – a long yellowish white root which resembled a carrot and smelled very definitely like horseradish. We took it home and I asked my mother to determine whether or not we had discovered a wild horseradish patch. She confirmed our find and armed with a shovel and a grape basket we returned to the Barnes' front yard.

We had dug only two or three roots when Mrs. Barnes questioned us and issued a desist order. After dark that evening, we sneaked back, filled our chip basket with muddy roots and, in the process, completely wrecked that front yard.

We were in business. Our goal was to make gallons and gallons of prepared horseradish which we could readily sell to the neighbors at five cents a glass. We began operations in the kitchen but were soon "urged" to leave. So the back porch became our factory. Bobby suggested that maybe we should wash the radishes before we attempted to grate them. I vetoed this suggestion with the explanation that, even though a great deal of mud was clinging to the roots, we could wash it off after grating. This, I argued, would speed up the operation. I sneaked the cheese grater out of the kitchen and we took turns rubbing the radish and our hands on the sharp projections of this metal torture device.

Results were frustrating. After seriously damaging our fingers and obtaining about a thimble full of grated radish and mud we resorted to dicing with a rusty knife, using the back door step as a cutting board. We cut up about ten of the roots into pea-sized pieces. Bobby again suggested that now might be a propitious point in our manufacturing program to wash the product. I argued against it, pointing out that the pea-sized cubes were entirely too big to be pickled for use as a condiment, and first we must find a method of mincing the horse radish.

10

As our meat grinder was not available, we procured the heavy, short-handled ice cracking mallet and, while Bobby pounded, I kept the brown mess piled up on the wooden step for each succeeding blow. This operation was, in all probability, the forerunner of the power driven hammer mill.

An empty olive bottle and a discarded glass teacup, minus handle, were found in a corner of the pantry and the gooey mass was scraped into them. We had apparently lost a sizeable quantity in the pounding process, through splatter and absorption into the step and the face of the mallet, for now we found that there was barely enough to fill the cup and cover the bottom of the bottle. But, both of us being fair minded, we proportioned the goo equally into the two containers. One to be sold to Bobby's mother and one to mine. Bobby recommended that, at this point in the process, it would be proper to rinse the horseradish. But I had already brought out the bottle of vinegar and had doused the contents of the olive bottle with it. So we filled the cup too. I remember my defensive remark. "Well, the vinegar makes it brown anyway." We tore off squares of newspaper and tied them in place over the tops of the receptacles.

The end result of our condiment venture was two half-filled "glasses" of a murky brown substance, not as dark as bread crumbs soaked in coffee, more like uncooked oatmeal and tea. Our original massive production dream was greatly diminished. But these two samples were just trial balloons anyway and would prove the market possibilities.

We decided then and there, that when production got up to full volume in the next day or so, we would buy several dozen new, quart Mason jars and perhaps raise the price to ten cents.

Bobby's mother ordered him out of the house when he tried to sell his bottle to her. My mother bought the glass cup and contents after commenting "It's a bit dark looking Jack, but it does smell like the real thing, even through the paper top."

11

The following day, while trying to help out the chickens, by retrieving a piece of cantaloupe rind from the old open topped flour barrel that served as a garbage container at our back door, I came across the teacup of horseradish, complete with newspaper top still intact.

Oh well we tried.

NUMBER 101 AND 102
(Circa 1899)

With Authorization

Common Knowledge: And then there was the time when I was about six years old when the desirability and advantages of big business, mass production and large scale operations first became apparent to me. We, Father, Mother, Bert and I were in Newark visiting uncle Tom and Aunt Libby. Les, my oldest cousin, who at that time was about eighteen, was imbued with the idea that anything worth doing was worth doing, not necessarily well but big.

Hearsay: Les was interested in horses and their welfare, carriage horses, bakery and milk wagon horses, show horses, race horses, dray[2] horses and horse car horses.

From Cousin Marion – she was a little snooper: Unfortunately the only ones in any of these categories with which Les could openly claim prime responsibility were his father's delivery wagon horse and his father's carriage horse: a beautiful animal, stabled in the barn behind Uncle Tom's residence on Seventh Street. But there were other horses committed to his care which he didn't care to admit.

From Les himself: Promptly at five o'clock each morning, six days a week, Les was permitted to feed and water Hannibal, wash his face, brush his mane and harness him to the single seated runabout and then jump into the carriage and drive ceremoniously to the kitchen door a distance of some forty feet from the carriage house. Tom would appear precisely at five forty-five, roll his fat little torso into the runabout, take the reins from Les without a word, dismiss Les with a curt nod of his balding head, tilt his little black derby jauntily over his left ear, shift the protruding toothpick from the on to the off side of his mouth and slapping the reins on Hannibal's rump would ride out onto Seventh

---

[2] A large, powerful horse used to pull heavy loads.

Street and turn right for the half-mile ride to his prosperous little butcher shop.

From the little snooper: Les, as was his custom, would soon take off, (presumably to high school) with an assortment of school books under his arm, these to confirm his mother's trust. Actually, Les was on his way to Gordon's livery stable where Mr. Gordon allowed him to cater to the wants of the horses. I never learned whether Mr. Gordon paid Les a small stipend for this service or not.

From Aunt Libby, proud of her son's initiative: A simple medication which Mr. Gordon was prone to use for scratches abrasions, harness sores - or ankle bruises on any of the horses entrusted to his care was petrolatum or petroleum jelly - (grease to me.) Les' mother was a firm believer in arnica[3] for the relief of sprains, painful joints and pulled muscles. Les, considering the advantages of both of these panaceas hit upon the proposition that if both of these items were good for ailments a combination of the two would be far superior to either alone.

From the little snooper: Following his bent for doing things in a big way, Les arranged to purchase (on the cuff) a fifty pound keg of petrolatum and in like manner to obtain a quart of tincture of arnica from the corner apothecary. He was obliged to obtain the arnica in eight ounce bottles and so he, in order to allay suspicion, made four trips to the store, spacing the visits at three day intervals and arranging to alternate his purchases between Dr. Sampson and Mr. Dukes the owner and clerk respectively. This procedure was followed because he did not want to arouse his father's suspicion when the statement from the druggist was received at home. His father would of course pay it without question, but a single item of four dollars would be more likely to arouse his father's curiosity than four one dollar items. Besides he might, of necessity, have to dig up the $2.50 from his own resources to pay for the grease.

---

[3] A genus of perennial, herbaceous plants in the sunflower family used to prepare anti-inflammatory preparations (used mostly for bruises).

14

From Aunt Libby (she boasted about her son's cleverness in adding an extra 100 wagons to his fleet): Les mixed the arnica with the petrolatum, used it copiously on the cuts and bruises of the livery stable horses and was so well pleased with the apparent results that he decided to go into the horse medicine business on a big scale of course. He "borrowed" an old bakery wagon from behind the stable, had a sign painted for it on a piece of oilcloth. The exact wording of the sign I don't remember, but for expediency let's call it Dr. Atchason's Horse Remedies, and then, not to belittle this imposing venture, he painted the number 101 on the outside of the dashboard of the wagon. The oilcloth sign was easily attached, with twine, to the right hand (curb) side of this impromptu delivery van. It looked very professional.

From the little snooper: He finally purchased (again on the cuff) the old bakery wagon and admitted, as a partner, a young man, who was also a high school dropout, but who had access to a dilapidated wagon complete with motive power and harness. This second van was appropriately numbered 102.

From who else? – the little snooper: These two salesmen then individually visited all neighborhood stables and dispensed their wares at a fair profit. It so happened that the first batch of salve ran out at the same time that an inquisitive veterinarian read the sign on No. 101 and pursued an investigation by the authorities, peddling without a license or purporting to be a veterinary doctor or some other such ridiculous charge. This misfortune also happened just at the time when Les was negotiating for six more kegs of grease and a wholesale price on arnica. Needless to say, the sales were culminated and Les took up an interest in picture show ownership, management and operation. But that's a different story and I am not well versed in that big venture except to remember that it too crashed.

THE NIGHT THE BELL FELL
(February 5, 1900)

And then there was the time of the raging fire in St. John's Church. Bedlam, confusion, almost hysteria in our household. I had Just returned home from Miss Curtiss' kindergarten when the ominous sound of that Franklin Fire Department bell rang out over our quiet little town. A hurried phone call placed by Maggie DeWoody[4] to the operator, revealed that our church was on fire.

My father, although thoroughly acclimated to refinery fires, was upset to no end as he rode up on his bicycle. This was something else again. He was distraught, ordered my mother to gather up us kids and follow him down Liberty Street to the scene of the conflagration. He had most likely received word of the fire through someone at his office and immediately pedaled home. "Those fire fighters will need hot coffee, plenty of hot coffee." He grabbed the little brown, wooden coffee mill by the crank and set out on his cycle through the center of town towards St. John's Church.

My mother bundled me up in my little sailor overcoat and led Bert and me in hasty pursuit of my father. Maggie trailed on after us, wringing her hands and calling on the Savior to make the fire to please go out. Although she was a member in good standing of the Evangelical Church, she also favored our church.

We arrived at the church amid confusion. My mother immediately took me into the rectory and recommended that I was to stay there. People were everywhere, the fire engine was wheezing and puffing at the curb at the side of the burning church. Firemen and "helpful" citizens were rushing aimlessly about, dragging hose and church furniture into hopeless confusion in the church yard.

---

[4] Maggie DeWoody is listed in the 1900 United States Federal Census as a servant in the George Stansbury household. She would have been 32 years old in 1900.

I lost contact with brother Bert, but he was two years my senior and was not confined to the rectory as I was. Basil, Hubert and Cyril Judge were stationed at the front church entrance. They had, probably, also been instructed to "stay." Mrs. Judge conducted me to the second floor living room of the rectory where I was met by Grace Judge and the two Moffat boys, all of whom were about my own age. We took turns in looking out the side window, where by craning our necks, we were just able to see the flames leaping from the roof over the chancel[5]. All in all it was not an advantageous place from which to supervise the progress of the fire.

Mother and Maggie had probably retreated to the rectory kitchen and were engaged in brewing coffee and making sandwiches for the exhausted firemen and on-lookers. By pressing my face against the window glass, I caught a glimpse of my father in the crowd below. He was busily engaged in helping to drag a pew down the front steps of the church.

How had the fire been started? A number of theories were advanced by my fellow observers. Perhaps Mrs. Trunkey had set it on fire to chase the devil out of the basement. Perhaps Mr. Hanna, who had been plugging for a new church, had arranged it. The question was resolved when it was explained by Grace, that two men, who had been employed to clean the dust from the pipe chamber of the organ, had pushed over a candle, used by them to light their work, and the dust had flashed up giving the two men just time enough to retreat to safety.

But the title of this episode is "The Night the Bell Fell." I've gone far off the subject, but for a good reason. I had been taken home by Maggie DeWoody and safely tucked into bed by the time the bell made it's last stand and I report that incident by hearsay. George Allen's calm and true story of the bell's last gasp. It seems that the building itself was lost and most of the firemen and even many of the spectators

---

[5] Chancel: the part of a church near the altar, reserved for the clergy and choir, and typically separated from the nave by steps or a screen.

had lost interest in the dying embers. My mother and father had long since returned home. Only George and a few of his cohorts remained at the scene when, as George related, a fierce crackling of smoldering beams was heard. A shower of sparks from the, still standing, belfry much like those emanating from a skyrocket lighted up the front yard of the church. George told that he knew the bell was coming down and his first impulse was to look above the shower of sparks to verify the fact that the bell was coming down, not going up. Then a glum cracking of timbers released the bell and it hurtled to the stone floor of the entrance way, giving off one last doleful bong as it reached it's final place of rest, amid the half burned studs and charcoal of the remnants of the once beautiful church.

The following Sunday, services were held in a second floor court room of the Venango County court house, and this resulted in a forced vacation of many weeks for me from attending the regular Sunday services.

I remember standing on the, front bench of this unfamiliar court of justice and vigorously counting the windows in the room. The church service was being read at the time but it held little interest for me. I was counting. I stood on that bench at the front of that large room, with windows on three sides and proceeded with my count. I emphasized each count with a gesture of my right arm, pointing my finger at each window as I counted it.

There were seventeen windows in that chamber of justice, as I remember. That's quite a few for a kindergarten student to count. But my method of arriving at a reasonable total was simple. There were six windows in each of the two side walls of the room and five in the rear. All that was required of me was that I count each side wall and the rear separately and remember these three numbers. Then, at the first opportunity, repeat them to mother and, quick as a flash, she added them for me.

Oh shucks! I meant to tell you about the night that the bell fell. But I've already done that. Haven't I?

THE DAY I FIRST MET HARRY
(Circa 1900)

And there was the time when I was walking up the alley which paralleled Liberty on the south. I noticed a boy of about my own age, six to seven, seated on the wooden fence in back of Plummer's house. "Oh I say sir," called this boy, "you don't happen to have a piece of string on you do you?" I turned to see who the "sir" was and realizing that there was no one else in the immediate neighborhood, I came to the conclusion that the "sir" was addressed to me.

I hesitatingly said, "Hi," and assured him that he was correct in his assumption that I did not have a piece of string on me. "What you want it for?" I asked.

"Oh," sez he, "I'm making a rabbit trap and I need a long piece of string to snap it with, Come here and I'll show you." I edged to the fence where he was perched and by standing on tip toe was able to peer over into the garden. Nothing but cabbages, row after row of nothing but cabbages, In the middle of this extensive garden of cabbages was a wooden box, tilted on edge with it's open side down, and held in this position by a foot long strip of cedar shingle with a short length of clothes line knotted around it.

"See," says my new acquaintance, "I put some cabbage leaves under the box and then lie down out of sight and when a rabbit goes under the box to eat them leaves, I pull the string and the box traps him. "But I need a longer rope, so's I can get out of sight better." - I considered that I had met up with a genius, although it did puzzle me a bit to get the rabbit's way of thinking. Why would he go under the box to eat a few wilted cabbage leaves when the whole garden of fresh green ones was at his disposal? Another thing, which did not occur to me until later, was how to get an elusive bunny from under an upturned box.

We talked for a few minutes. I complimented him on his ingenuity and he must have admired me, for hadn't he called me "sir"? I suggested that he walk home with me, I was sure that I could find a

19

long piece of string there. We walked and he talked. His name was Harry Henderson. He and his mother had just yesterday moved from Erie into the Plummer home. Some sort of a business arrangement between his mother and Mrs. Plummer.

I went into the pantry and dragged out that bottom junk drawer, the habitat of surplus of everything wanted, but mostly unwanted items. Left over parts from years and years of unproductive mechanical effort. No string, not a piece longer than a shoelace was to be found. Then an idea popped into my anxious head and I led the disappointed Harry out to the screened back porch where Carl Read had left his comparatively new willow fishing pole, complete with hook, line and bobber. The hook was tied to one end of the line which was stretched from the tip of the pole to the bark-skinned end which served as a handle. About twenty feet of line was tightly wrapped around this handle. After trying vainly to untie the line from the hook, Harry and I took the whole tackle out to the big rock in the back yard and pounded the line with a small stone until it was cut about six inches above the olive bottle cork bobber. We unwound the line from the handle, put the rod, hook and bobber under the front porch, for security reasons (out of sight, out of mind) and returned to the cabbage patch, where we tied the line to the end of the trigger string and then we both lay down on our bellies in the garden mud and waited for the rabbit to come and signal us to pull the trigger. After about an hour of fruitless watching we gave up and I went home.

Next morning, before I had finished breakfast, brother Bert informed me that a strange boy was standing, sitting and climbing on the pipe fence in our front yard. Immediately, I conjectured, it must be Harry. It was. He said the trap had been sprung during the night and suggested that I go with him to get the rabbit. Here was a problem. How do you retrieve a scared but active bunny from under an upturned soap box? Harry admitted that he did not know. But on our way to the cabbage patch he related how his uncle Bernie had once reached under such an upturned box and a skunk had greeted him. Who had pulled the trigger string? Were we confident that the rabbit, (if it was a rabbit,) had tripped the trigger from inside the box? Harry didn't know and I was sure that I didn't. I dreamed up more and more wild possibilities as we hastened to the trap site.

Then suddenly our problems were solved, Ralphie Evans appeared at our side and joined us as we jogged down the alley. "Where you going? What you gonna do?" These were questions readily answered by Harry. We entered the garden from the rear. Sure enough the box was down. I took my position at the end of the fishing line. I felt responsible for its safe return to Carl's fishing rod. Harry, after instructing Ralphie how to raise the box and grab the quarry, took up his original position straddling the fence explaining to us that if the rabbit should elude Ralphie's grasp, he, Harry, would be in excellent position and in readiness to point out just which way the rabbit had run. A stupid advantage if I ever heard one.

Ralphie approached the upturned box cautiously, knelt beside it and as instructed, tilted it and thrust his arm beneath it. He repeated this action three times without result. Then, throwing caution to the wind, he stood up and kicked the box over on it's side. It was empty. You expected a skunk? So did I.

The trap was a failure! I gathered up the fishing line and retreated towards home, leaving Ralphie to "ooh" and "ahh" in wonderment at the versatility of my new found friend, Harry.

TAMBOURINE VIRTUOSO
(Circa 1900)

And then there was the time when Shorty Evans invited me to accompany him to a young men's meeting in the St. John's parish house.[6]

We walked down Liberty Street to the church, a matter of some four or five blocks. Seemed to me like that many miles, for Shorty insisted that I be privileged to carry the case containing his cornet. The cornet was of average size and weight, but the case had apparently been designed for a small piano. It kept bumping against my knees and swinging in the most perturbing arcs – first it would crack me on the right knee and then swing violently and catch me on the back of the upper calf of the same leg.

I tried cradling the case in both arms in front of me, like a doting father might carry an injured child. I tried right shoulder arms. I tried slope arms and present arms with that unwieldy case. No advantage except to make my arms ache.

Shorty was, apparently, totally unconscious of my discomforts, for he strolled on, whistling happily and at times commenting on the great number of dogs who saw fit to rush to their front gates as we approached, bark furiously and, probably due to Shorty's nonchalance and musical whistle, subside with an energetic wagging of tail.

I was young and proud of the trust placed in me by my more mature companion. So I was not tempted to suggest that he carry the case for a few steps.

Finally we arrived at the parish house. I parked the cornet case in the areaway leading to the basement assembly room. Fifty or sixty folding chairs had been arranged in a wide arc, facing the platform. Six other boys were already there when Shorty and I arrived, and at four-thirty, two more straggled in. Then the Reverend Martin Aigner

---

[6] GHS II himself states that this is "Substantially true / plus a bit of fluff."

appeared and informed us that our speaker for the meeting had undoubtedly missed his train in Meadville, thus we would dispense with the assembly for today.

There were only ten of us present. Perhaps the missing members of the order were unconcerned about this "get together" as the guest speaker seemed to be. Missed his train at Meadville? Phooey, the only possible diversion of which Meadville could boast was to stand in the depot train shed and watch the "switchies" casually assemble the three cars for the Franklin Branch limited. Twenty minutes or so after the train was complete, the station master would announce it's departure, and within the next hour the Franklin Branch would actually be on its way.

The Rev. Mr. Aigner gave us a short lecture on the evils of "borrowing" that which was not ours. – It seems his son Francis had misplaced his pocket knife during the last session of Sunday school, and the whole membership was looked upon with suspicion. Mr. Aigner repeatedly used the word "purloined" in his lecture. I remembered it particularly, for until then, I had not the faintest notion of it's meaning. Fact is, I had never heard the word before. He then touched on the wages of sin and dismissed us.

Shorty and I strolled up Liberty Street. This time I declined the honor of nursing the cornet, so Shorty slung it over his shoulder and resumed his whistling.

At Pop Martin's candy store, we paused and feasted our eyes on the window display. Shorty assured me that he would like to buy a string of rock candy but had thoughtlessly left his purse at home.

As we approached Thirteenth Street, we heard music. A small group of people had gathered to listen to the five piece Salvation Army band. This band was composed of an accordionist, one trumpeter, one trap drummer, one base drummer and a saxophone player, who did double duty, when time permitted, with a broken-down tambourine.

Shorty elbowed his way to the front of the group of spectators and I followed close behind him. Lieutenant Sherman was now appealing for more volunteers to play in his band. He saw that my

23

companion was carrying an instrument case and paused his dissertation long enough to ask what it contained. Shorty told him it was a cornet but that he was still taking lessons and couldn't play very well. This was an honest but unexpected admission on Shorty's part. This didn't prove a deterrent to the Lieutenant who insisted that Shorty come over to the firehouse on the following evening at seven o'clock and join in band practice.

We backed away from the fast dwindling assembly and Shorty quietly advised me that he wouldn't join unless I did also. "But I can't play," sez I. Shorty thought for a moment and then came up with the suggestion that I would beat the base drum. This idea did not appeal to me particularly, and beside Harry Wilson, the little fat man, already had the base drum assignment, would be out of a job if I should be appointed to the base drum chore. I appealed to Shorty's sense of fairness concerning this fact.

"Oh he won't be out of a job," says Shorty, "Lieutenant Sherman is his uncle and besides I've heard that Harry can play the piano." It puzzled me as to why my companion would bring up Harry's ability on the piano. For a piano, I figured, would not be a convenient instrument to lug on a tour of Liberty Street. But I didn't want to beat the base drum anyway, so I let the subject drop.

Shorty had an inspiration – "How's for you to play the tambourine?" he suggested. I demurred with the comment that the tambourine was not a musical instrument and furthermore I had no idea how to shake it anyway. "Of course it's musical," countered Shorty, "and I can learn you how to play it in practically no time at all, come on."

We walked across the street toward Rollya's stationery store. Rollya's was called a stationery store but it was more like an emporium, for they displayed everything from Ju-Ju-Bees to wash boards. Reba, the fourteen year old daughter of the Rollya family, was standing at the front entrance of the store. She was apparently in complete charge of the sales for the time being. As we walked across the street, Shorty

24

instructed me in what I was to do when we arrived at the store. "You go inside and away to the back and ask the price of fishing reels."

"But I don't want to buy a fishing reel," I protested, "and besides I haven't got a nickel."

"You ain't supposed to buy," whispered Shorty, "just look at 'em and ask how much." We greeted Reba and I hurried to the rear of the store, following instructions, where the sporting goods were available. Reba, like a dutiful saleslady followed me, while Shorty stopped just inside the front door and bustled himself thumbing through some magazines.

Following directions, I pointed to a very elaborate reel in the showcase and asked, "How much is this one?"

Reba retrieved the reel, looked at the price tag and said "A dollar fifty." I never dreamed that a fishing reel could possibly cost so much. I blushed and pointed to a simple little winder that had no fancy doodads. Reba says, "twenty five cents." I turn and stumble back out of the store, mumbling that this one was just what I wanted and that I would come back tomorrow to buy it. Shorty had retreated to the sidewalk and was fumbling with the catch of his cornet case.

We walked up Liberty Street towards home. Finally coming to the Nursery Club[7]. There we seated ourselves on the wooden steps of the front porch and had just gotten comfortable when a carriage drove up to the stepping stone and several ladies alighted and approached the club. Shorty and I took stock of our position and concluded that we might be in the way, so we ambled across the yard to Colonel Lewis's house and reclined on the Colonel's front steps. Shorty then produced, from the cumbersome case, a shiny bright pie tin with the inscription 5¢

---

[7] The Nursery Club was a social fellowship resulting from the merger of social clubs in 1879. The organization purchased the property at 1340 Liberty Street in Franklin, PA., adding a grand ballroom, billiard room and other amenities. It was renamed the Franklin Club in 1913 and was the social center of downtown Franklin, PA for many years. In 2009 the property was restored to its original luster and used as a restaurant and event space.

marked on the bottom in the most brilliant scarlet crayon which I had ever seen.

This pie tin, I learned, was a simulated tambourine. It had no jingles but was approximately the proper size, and when Shorty slapped it smartly against his knee, it produced a sound not unlike that of a tambourine. He handed the pan to me, showed me how to grasp it in my right hand and strike it crisply with the knuckles of my left. We arose and walked home, keeping step to Shorty's whistled version of "Rag Time Gal" and my bungling and erratic beat of the pie tin.

That evening I reviewed the happenings of the afternoon, especially as to just how we had come into possession of that brand new pie pan. Suddenly it dawned on my dense understanding – Shorty had filched it at Rollya's. He had admitted, when we were looking in the candy store window, that he had no money, and he had not spoken to Reba, the sales girl, after entering the store so he could not possibly have arranged credit. I had been a dupe, a pawn, a patsy. While I was in the sporting goods department, Shorty had picked up the pan from the kitchen wares and sneaked it out.

Even though the price was only a nickel, and he had presumably swiped it to further my musical talent, and had, in fact, given it to me, it was stolen property and my conscience couldn't tolerate my owning that which was tinged with fraud. That work "purloined" kept popping into my mind, and Mr. Aigner had defined purloined as a sin. I considered giving it back to Shorty or even taking it back to the store and surreptitiously slipping it into the stack of pans that was on the shelf near the entrance. Neither of these solutions appealed to me, too much explanation was involved in the first, too much risk and hazard in the second, and besides, that pan had been rather severely dented from my ardent attempts to make it sound musical.

I slipped out of the house as the sun was disappearing in the trees behind the second clearing, the pan partially concealed in my blouse. I made my way up Sixteenth Street, sneaked unseen under the grape arbor of Read's house. Then taking careful aim, I sailed the pan at Shorty's

26

house, hoping to bury it in the weeds, which, in lieu of flowers, surrounded the front porch.

The Evans' house was a two story frame dwelling, situated on a somewhat level lot at the top of a fifteen foot terrace, at the base of which I was now cringing. The bathroom was, of necessity, on the ground floor because the spring and gravity fed water supply could only afford a measly trickle on the upper level.

The pan sailed in a beautiful arc, the last rays of the setting sun glinting on the shiny tin plate and the red crayon 5¢ mark, not yet completely erased by contact with my aching knuckles, gleamed like a ruby in the center of the flying plate.

The trajectory was a bit high and the missile flew smoothly through the partially open window of the Evan's bathroom. I heard it bounce against the far wall and then clatter to a stop into the old zinc bathtub.

I disappeared into the evening as quietly as a zephyr and reached home almost before that bouncing pan had come to rest. I believe that an all time speed record was established that day, down the Sixteenth Street hill.

What a worried and sleepless night I had, wondering what the reaction would be on the morrow. Would I be ostracized from polite society? Would Mr. Evans appear at our dining room table while I was eating breakfast and demand an explanation of just why my tambourine was found in his bathtub or would Shorty simply beat me up?

Surprisingly, no repercussions were apparent on the following day. Shorty was his usual musical self and made no reference to the pie pan which had doubtless by now, been retrieved from the tub, nor was the subject of the Salvation Army band touched upon again.

Needless to say, I never did attain the status of a concert tambourinist. Truth is, I am, even now, a trifle allergic to any kind of pie.

THAT MAGNIFICENT SHOE BUTTON MACHINE
(Circa 1900)

And then there was the time when my mother took me down town with her. She was going to the shoe store, presumably to purchase for herself, a pair of those, then in style, high button shoes. It must have been Saturday afternoon for she had told me that she had, under pressure, asked Anna Myers to meet her and help her decide whether to get plain or fancies. Anna was at liberty only on Saturday afternoons, but Anna thought that Anna's opinion was highly valued, especially on shoe styles.

We entered the Charles Harris Shoe Store. Anna had not yet arrived, and when mother sat down, I busied myself with studying the shoe button machine. It was a rather complex, three legged, iron device of someone's ingenuity, standing about waist high and was used for the one purpose of fastening shoe buttons to the leather uppers of ladies shoes. The buttons were fed into a magazine by the handful. The shoe was held under the stitcher by the operator, who then tramped on a pedal and the button was firmly clamped into the shoe leather. I naturally had to try it out in stamp on the pedal a few times. Every downward push of the panel was accentuated by a metallic clang and a perfectly clamped button would fall to the floor. I wasn't fixing shoes, I was just investigating.

Mr. Harris suggested, in a nice way, I desist. Mother then gave me a penny and recommended that I go out onto Thirteenth Street and look in the store windows, "But don't go across the street."

I skipped out, happy with my so quickly earned fortune. There was nothing up Liberty Street to interest me except Grandpa Allen's sunken front yard with the elevated walkway to the porch, which I had seen a million times. So I walk down Thirteenth Street pass the uninteresting windows of Woodburn, Cone and Steele's big store. Passed a number of lesser store's windows when nothing caught my fancy.

Then joyfully I approach that Pulver Gum Co.'s chewing gum slot machine which was firmly affixed to the entrance of John Riesenman's drugstore. I have a decision to make, the two plungers of the machine were staring at me like bulging eyeballs. The function of the one on the right was to drop a stick of gum into the pocket below the plungers. The left one would deliver a teentsy bar of chocolate in the same pocket - that is, provided a penny had first been inserted in the slot. I chose the gum side, and to make sure that all was in order, I pushed the right hand plunger gingerly before I risked my penny.

Everything seemed to be satisfactory - the plunger plunged smoothly and returned to the set position when released. I contributed my one, and only, cent and pushed again. Nothing responded, no gum, no chocolate, no nothing - just those two nickel plated eyeballs leering at me. I pushed again and again, I even pushed the chocolate plunger a half dozen times, nothing, I was dismayed and frantic.

Also, so unobservant that I wasn't even aware of the interest I had built up among four or five boys of about my own age, who were clustered around me as I stared back at those two protruding eyes. The boys were friendly and offered suggestions and took turns pushing in the plungers.

Ray Blakely, a recent acquaintance of mine, (met him just about a week ago at a session of Miss Curtis' kindergarten) recommended, after poking a few times on those plungers, that I go into the drugstore and complain to the management. They would undoubtedly make full restitution of my financial loss or perhaps send the man out to fix the machine.

I demurred - I wasn't much at approaching a strange man in the store, much less of attempting to state a grievance or demanding compensation. Finally Ray convinced me that I should go in and ask. He even volunteered to accompany me on this hazardous mission. So in we went. I hung back behind Ray when the clerk asked cheerily, "Well boys what can I do for you?"

Ray, without hesitation explained the whole unfortunate situation, ending with, "And he wants his money back." Which remark, I deduced at the time was not the right statement for him to have made under the circumstances.

But, much to my astonishment, the man apparently did not take offense. He explained, in some detail, that the store had nothing to do with the slot machine except to provide it shelter in the doorway. As he said nothing about a refund, Ray and I retreated to the place of frustration and the, now a larger, circle of boys surrounding that popeyed machine. Word had of that evidently gotten out that one of their kind had made contract with this slot machine and the machine had reneged and failed to deliver. It did not register with me that I could have mentioned my close acquaintance with Mr. Riesenman, the store's owner, and probably have immediately gotten my money back. But, to be shamefully honest, in the uncertainty of my predicament, I didn't even realize that it was my next door neighbor's store.

The boys were still grouped around the machine. Staring back at those two metal eyeballs and occasionally taking a vicious punch at one or both of them.

Down the street came Jimmy Carnes, his empty Franklin Evening News carrier bag hanging loosely from his shoulder. He paused, question one of the onlookers, nodded understandingly, then wormed his way to the front of the stage, gave that right hand plunger a tremendous swap with his open hand. That gum machine must have realized that it had at last met its master, for it delivered a wrapped stick of gum to the pick-up pocket.

Jimmy had scarcely slowed down in his hurried walk along Thirteenth Street but he had accomplish the impossible in that brief instant. He was gone before I could thank him. It flashed through my ever active brain that I should break the gum into two pieces and offer him the lesser of the two. But gee, he was gone now and I wasn't about to cause a furor and call attention to myself by racing after him. And two, that little stick of gum looked distressingly small - what would it look like if I broke it in half?

The boys had broken up now and had gone on their various ways to find other friends in trouble. I put the gum in my mouth and hurried back to the shoe store where my mother and Anna were talking in the entrance way, so I couldn't go back into this store and stamp on the treadle of that fabulous button machine now. Mother had apparently made her purchase and I was not about to go in without her. I wondered why some mechanical devices, like that complex shoe button machine were so trouble-free while others, such as that much simpler, dispenser could be so frustrating.

BARING MY SOUL
(Circa 1900-1903)

---- Just a few of my early, really embarrassing moments. ----

And then there was the time when I was in grade one of the Second Ward School. The teacher had read us a story in which the three children Johnny, Mary and Beatrice were cavorting with a doll and a rabbit in the apple orchard. We were asked to volunteer to advise the rest of the class of something which any one of the characters in the story might do if not confined to the text. One girl raised her hand and reported that Mary picked a basket of apples, another girl asserted that Beatrice ate one of the apples from Mary's basket. I raised my hand and pronounced, very convincingly, that the rabbit ran up one of the apple trees. There followed a burst of laughter and the teacher informed me that this was not the usual behavior of a bunny. I quickly recovered my composure and allowed that the rabbit had run down a hole. - Oh well!

And then there was the time in Josephine Grant's get-together class for us neighborhood boys when papa Grant had taken over the class to relieve his daughter from too much pandemonium. He had told us about the fearless animals and wondered if any of us could tell him what use could be put to the ivory tusks of an elephant. Grinny Read immediately responded that ivory was used in the manufacture of piano keys. Son Dennison, with more worldly contacts, assured us that ivory was also used in making billiard balls. A lull in the proceedings prompted me to venture that ivory was of prime importance in the making of Ivory soap. Laughter - but this time I was unable to provide an alternative. - Oh well!

And then there was the time on Christmas morning when Ralph Evans presented me with a little crockery bank in the form of a monkey sitting on a stump. Ralph's big brother LeRoy (Shorty) at the same time gave Bert a duplicate, from the same mold, only mine was glazed brown and Bert's was green. The first presentation ceremony (Ralph's to me) was scarcely completed when Ralph demanded, expectantly, "Jimmy what did you get for me?"

I was abashed; I hadn't gotten him anything, but my ever alert mind came to the rescue, and I responded, "Ralph I didn't buy you anything for Christmas but you otta see what I've got you for Easter!" - Oh well!

And then there was the time, on the day before my sixth birthday, when Maggie DeWoody asked me which I would rather have - six nickels or a half a dollar. I promptly answered, six nickels. But in a consultation with brother Bert, he assured me that a half dollar was far more valuable than six nickels and tried to explain the difference to me. I don't know whether he was having trouble with his arithmetic or I was following my customary hard headed stupidity. I couldn't properly understand that a fifty-cent piece could have greater value than the six promised nickels. On the following day I was given the half-dollar anyhow, and it served me in good stead. Or did it? Before I had the opportunity to lose it, Maggie, her brother and I drove down to the DeWoody farm.

One of my most sincere desires was to own a buggy whip of my very own, for what reason I cannot say, except that I wanted it. We stopped at the general store on our half-day journey and low-and-behold the center of attraction in this little country store was a display of buggy whips - a circular, rotatable stand from which were suspended a dozen or more carriage whips, all priced at fifty cents. I rotated the stand time and time again until the storekeeper approached and suggested that I desist. In spite of my mentor's protests and before the half dollar could burn a hole in my pocket or otherwise disappear, I carefully selected a whip from the rack, turned my money over to the storekeeper, swished the whip a few times, climbed back into the buggy and in the next mile or two had lost the whip. At any rate, it was not among my paraphernalia when we drove into the DeWoody barn lot. But a person can't have everything, and besides the pleasure I got from buying the whip. I recalled the several good swishes I gave it in front of the store on our way back to the carriage to continue our journey. - Oh well!

And then there was the time in the post office when I was asked by Mrs. Smith, a close friend of Colonel Lewis to let her see that wonderful gold watch, which she understood the Colonel had given me. (Bert got one also.) I eagerly, but clumsily fumbled in my watch pocket for the watch and finally brought it out for her inspection, remarking, due to my lack of dexterity in producing it, "I should otta have a fob."[8]

Mrs. Smith looked at the watch, and with a consoling reply to my concern about not having a fob, said, "Oh that will come later." - completely misunderstanding my motive in mentioning the lack of a fob. Guess it wasn't until late in the afternoon that the Colonel heard that those two Stansbury boys were two of the most unappreciative little brats that she had ever known. - Oh well!

And then there was the time when Elou McCalmont had invited me, among others, to play tennis on her uncle's court. When the game had progressed to the point where the players were supposed to change sides, I, showing off, didn't deem it proper for me to walk around the net, as the others had done. I nonchalantly attempted to jump the net. My heel caught in the supporting rope from which the net was suspended. I regained my equilibrium before I hit the ground but the net was not so agile, neither was one of the lathe-turned supporting wooden posts which broke off at the base. I assured Elou that the post must have been rotted at the lower extremity. This did not ease my conscience nor eliminate my guilty feeling for the bad jump. Repairs were impossible, but gee how I tried! Needless to say, that ended the tennis match for the day and probably for many days to follow. - Oh well!

---

[8] A short ribbon or chain attached to a watch and hanging out of the pocket in which the watch is kept.

NOW HEAR THIS
(Circa 1901)

You are probably familiar with the initial stage experiences of such great public idols as Maude Adams, John Gilbert, the Barrymores and many others. But are you familiar with the details of the first public appearance of your accomplished brother George? Well listen and be advised. This is the story.

It was a memorable highlight of my early education, a triumph which I didn't relish at the time and have avoided mentioning for several decades. Now some sixty-odd years later I no longer hesitate to talk.

Miss Alice Brady's first-grade class room was the scene. Charley Cummings and I occupied the front row double desk on the teacher's right hand. Possibly the geographical position of Charley's and my desk was responsible for the fate that I was chosen to take part in the Valentine Day ceremonies. My desk mate was not selected because the other two of the three thespians in this very short skit were girls. Besides Charley wasn't pretty like me.

Each of us, George Stansbury, Merriam Thomas and another girl, whose name has escaped me, were given carefully written four line poems, several days before the gala event was to take place. We were also instructed by Miss Brady as to the proper gestures to accompany each of our four line recitations.

On the great day, the two girls and I took our places on the slightly elevated platform at the front of the first-grade class room. We stood side by side - I was on the right wing, Merriam in the center and the unidentified actress on the left wing. The poem (we were told) interpreted the beauty of a spring day, from the rising of the sun until the going down of the same.

My speech came first, for I was to depict the early morning sun of this festive day by clasping my hands over my head, thus making the semblance of a circle which framed my handsome face - which, I had been advised, represented the sun. Alice Brady was no casting director.

35

Imagine a skinny, bunny eared, frosty faced, timid little kid being chosen to represent the glorious springtime sun rising majestically over the horizon to illuminate a lovely pastoral scene. Even Charley Cummings would have better fitted the part.

Of course I was immediately stricken with the nausea brought on by stage fright. I looked down at my shoes, and after insistent suggestions from Miss Brady, clasped my hands in the prescribed manner and boldly launched into my recital. The four lines of the poem had been well memorized. Their meaning was not apparent to me, but the words had a swinging di-da - di-da ripple of cadence to them that was most comforting to my musical temperament.

Then that awful moment, a gray haze closed in on my brilliant mind and no words came from my open mouth. I was prompted by someone, I don't know who but suspect it was Merriam. (Imagine such genius, knowing your own four lines and being able to help me with mine!) The thought of her devotion to the success of the act cleared my head and I ventured confidently into my part.

Today I cannot recall the complete four line poem but I think the first two lines were:

The bright sun peeped out on a brand new day,
It beamed on fields of lush green hay.

My rendition of the first line was an astounding success, perfect in every way, though lacking in forcefulness and, I do recall that while I was speaking, I looked down at my shoes again and thought that they could have been improved by a bit of brushing. The first line now behind me, and overwhelmed by my own ability and mastery of the situation, I recklessly bolted to the second line, something like this:

It screamed on heels of much lean pay.

A deluge of snickers and giggles from· the audience, convinced me that, due to over confidence, I had bungled the second line. At Miss Brady's suggestion I was to begin again, from the start. This time my first line triumph could not be repeated. In fact, the first line again could not be remembered.

My sight became blurred. This time my compatriot Merriam did not attempt to rescue me. Don't believe I'd have heard her anyhow. I lowered the frame from around the rising sun and stared at my unpolished shoes; no thought now of trying to remember the words of that starting line of that poem with the delightful sing-song beat. No inspiration, no speech, no words, no prompting.

I was later informed that I hurriedly retreated to the safety of the cloak room, leaving my two fellow artists to finish the play and alone to accept the thunderous plaudits of our fellow students.

My mind was a blank from the instant that Alice Brady suggested, "George lets start again, from the beginning," until she rescued me from the depths, of the cloak room after the 'performance'.

All in all, the session, skit, act or entertainment was a triumphant success not for the art of poetry, not for the beauty of the acting but for a period of rollicking enjoyment for all those present, except me.

PETRIFIED
(Circa 1901)

And then there was the time when I was in Miss Alice Brady's First grade class in Franklin and she was called to Miss Burge's room, probably for a short conference.

Out of a clear blue sky, she chose me to sit at her desk and maintain order in the class until she returned. She mentioned to the students that she would be gone only for a short period of time and that they were all to keep their seats and remain quiet – "And do what George tells you." Then she left.

I was definitely proud of my sudden elevation to responsibility but also horrified at the possibility of dire consequences. I sat on teacher's chair and smiled benevolently at my newly acquired charges.

Everything was quiet and peaceful for a matter of, perhaps, two minutes. Then Arundel Brown, the gangling black boy[9] who sat in the back row of the class-room, tore a sheet of paper from his tablet and noisily proceeded to crunch it into a ball with his big black hands. Then he arose from his seat and staggered clumsily up the aisle towards me. His left shoe squeaked loudly as he approached with a squeak-clump, squeak-clump accompaniment. I probably turned white as I slumped, as inconspicuously as possible, into Miss Brady's chair. And then my supreme sense of responsibility took charge and mustering all the courage at my command, I spoke to Arundel in a nervous, high pitched voice. "Rendel, you are 'sposed to stay at your desk." He paid no attention to me, but came on to the front of the room, deposited the wadded ball of paper in the teacher's waste-basket at the side of my desk and squeak-clumped, squeak-clumped back to his place.

The other members of the class, with a few exceptions, tittered audibly. Arundel did not resume his seat. He tore another sheet of paper from his writing tablet, again crumpled it noisily in his hands and headed

---

[9] Franklin Public Schools were integrated in the 1870s.

38

squeak-clump, squeak-clump back to my desk and threw the wadded paper into the waste-basket.

He went through this operation, perhaps six times in all, to the accompaniment of the titterings and giggles of the class. I now had no recourse to words of admonition. I had failed miserably at that in my first attempt, so now I just slumped and tried to look nonchalant on each successive squeak-clump, squeak-clump of Arundel's comings and goings. Would Miss Brady never return?

Finally, when I had given up all hope of being rescued, she did come back, released me from my position of trust and inquired, "George did you have any trouble?"

I blurted out that every one was good "'ceptin' Rendel." Then I tried to imagine what dire punishment she would mete out to him, perhaps he would be put in stocks. I had seen a picture of criminals being subjected to that form of confinement in my brother's history book, but here the prisoners were New Englanders. I had no idea where New England was situated nor what foreign country was involved. But what would be an appropriate substitute for stocks for an offender in the United States?

Maybe she would suspend him by his tied thumbs from one of the four tee shaped gas jets that were used, on occasion, to light the first grade room, or perhaps, (remembering another picture which I had seen in another book) she would blindfold him and force him to kneel, like the Chinese vandals, at the edge of a precipice while another Chinaman with a broad bladed, curved sword made ready to whop off their heads and kick their bodies into the abyss. I remember thinking, at the time, that this last form of punishment was perhaps a trifle too severe for the infraction of rules which had been committed by Arundel. But I would leave final judgement to Miss Brady. I had told him to sit down and he had ignored me.

It was almost three fifteen, to late to start another lesson and Miss Brady sat at her desk and thumbed through a book, probably on various forms of punishment which might be applied to Arundel.

At closing time, the pencil blocks were passed and each of us replaced his or her pencil in the proper holes in the blocks. Then Miss Brady dismissed the class. Not a word of thanks to me for my supervisory efforts of the afternoon. Not a word of censure to Arundel for his misdemeanor.

We left the building – that tall gangling black boy and I, arm in arm – squeak-clunk, squeak-clunk, all the way to the front gate.

How forgiving kids can be.

MERRIMENT AT MCCALMONT'S
(Circa 1902)

And then there was the time I found a note similar to this on my schoolroom desk.

YOUR INVITED TO A PRTY
AT ELOUS HOUSE
AFTER SCHOOL FRIDY

There must have been at least twenty-five such invitations, carefully printed on Harry Henderson's brand new, used Christmas gift printing press. These little oblongs of pasteboard and/or brown paper, (Harry had used up all of his stock of cards after printing nine or ten and had to substitute pieces of paper, carefully torn from a large sugar sack) had been systematically placed, one at each desk, in Mrs. Bauman's second grade room at school.

The first period of class, the spelling lesson, was taken up mainly with a babble of whispered questions and answers between the scholars: "Are you going?" "Where's she live?" "I can't , Mother's gonna wash my hair," etc.

The following day, Bert and I hurried home from school and quickly dressed in our Sunday best. Then we wandered across the street to Elou McCalmont's home where we joined about ten of my classmates. Bert, who was in the fifth grade, had not received a printed invitation but was prevailed upon to share mine, which he did although somewhat reluctantly. We spoke to Elou, who returned our greeting with a fixed smile and a muttered hello. Elou was always smiling in an impersonal sort of way, her eyes indicating that her thoughts were many, many miles away.

Among the guests were Boyd Parks, Marie and Helen Wilson, both unrelated to Nettie. Charlie Cummings, Henry and Miriam Thomas. Helen, Marie's little sister, who had not yet reached school age, was

41

there by parental edict, for anywhere that the elder daughter went, there went Helen also. Harry Henderson who was, in all probability, the party sponsor, seemed to be in charge of amusements. He had marked out a hopscotch playing field on the wide expanse of the McCalmont's front porch and Anna Riesenman and Bobby Read, two of the immediate neighbors, were already engaged in a game when Bert and I arrived. Anna and Bobby were there as my personal guests. I reasoned that my invitation covered all of my close friends whether in the second grade of our school or not. The "Social Director" was not making a great deal of headway in mingling the guests. Most of us were seated on the front steps or languidly standing against the porch posts and wishing we were somewhere other than where we were. Elou was lost in the depths of the "Hostess" wicker rocker. She was not attempting to engage in conversations, just sitting there, unmindful of her guests and smiling, ever smiling with that patent far away smile.

Elou's mother burst out of the front door, dressed for a shopping spree. She pranced across the width of the porch and swarmed down the front steps before realizing that there was an unduly large number of well dressed children at her door step. She paused in embarrassment and turned to Elou. "Why Elou," she trilled, "are you having a party?" Elou gave no sign of having heard her mother. Just sat there in that massive chair and continued her putty like smile.

Harry Henderson came to the rescue and explained to Elou's mother that indeed Elou was having a party and he attempted introductions. Mrs. McCalmont brushed off the meetings with a wave of her hand. And then addressing our group at large with a puzzled smile she said, "Well I had no idea, but you children go ahead and have fun." Then she hurried out the front gate with a parting word that she had to get to town.

The party was not proving to be a roaring success despite Harry's efforts to renew our interest by salvaging an overstuffed rag doll from the front yard and tossing it from one to another, bean-bag fashion.

Mrs. McCalmont's appearance and her remarks solidified our suspicions that there would be no refreshments. Bert broke the ice by leaving for home without a word of apology. Anna Riesenman and Bobby Read followed, after giving me a cold stare which seemed to say, "So this is a party?" Boyd Parks attempted a "permission to leave" curtsy at Elou's throne and soon only about six of the guests, four boys and the two Wilson girls remained to continue the "hilarity."

Pleasure lagged, tension increased. The realization that no sandwiches were to be forthcoming, no cake, no ice cream, not even lemonade, dampened our spirits immeasurably. Even Harry, the self-appointed master of entertainment, and in all probability, the originator of the party was nonplussed. He finally appealed to Elou, still perched on her throne with that placid, meaningless smile plastered on her otherwise somber face. Elou apparently had no solution to the problem and had no interest in it anyhow.

Then Harry's eager eye fell on the white sheet which had been carefully draped over the six-legged Ping Pong table which was folded and was resting against the wall behind Elou's chair. This folding table, a recent acquisition of Elou's father, was the pride and joy of Mr. McCalmont. The game of Ping Pong had only recently been introduced to the elite of Franklin society and Mr. McCalmont frequently entertained his friends with a spirited game of Ping Pong on this "hand crafted" table on the front porch of his home.

Harry, after receiving a nod of permission from the "queen," removed the sheet from the table and snapped down the legs. Then the table was dragged to a position directly across the front door. One severely dented Ping Pong ball was reclaimed from the floor, hiding in a corner of the porch. This crippled ball was freely batted by hand on the table's smooth surface. No net was present nor were any paddles. These were probably securely locked in Mr. McCalmont's bedroom closet. We soon tired of this ball-batting diversion and Harry stood on the table and attempted, without success, to touch the porch ceiling with outstretched right hand.

43

Helen Wilson, tomboy that she was, mounted the table and assuming a bent knee position in the center of the table's smooth top, tried to leap high and brush the ceiling with her extended fingers. There followed a cracking, crunching sound and Helen's left leg disappeared through that smooth green table top. Helen was in a most embarrassing situation - her left leg was protruding below the table's surface, something like an added seventh leg. She was unable to extricate herself from this awkward and unladylike position. On Harry's recommendation, Charley Cummings and I attempted to tilt the table to the near side. Two of the spindly legs broke off and Helen was plummeted out of the trap and cascaded heels over head, down the porch steps.

Repairs to the table were out of the question. But those two broken legs wouldn't show if the table was again folded and that gaping hole in the smooth table top was not apparent when we draped the sheet over it and stood it in it's former place against the wall.

But the party was over. Elou's few remaining guests quietly melted into the landscape and pursued their various ways toward home. Elou was apparently neither disturbed nor distressed by the unhappy turn of events. She just sat there with her patent Mona Lisa smile throughout the whole affair. The party was not of her making. Harry had evolved the entire miserable affair and wished it on Elou.

Why should I have had a sense of guilt for the ruin of that Ping Pong table? I was only one of many invited and disappointed guests. But I remember that for the following few days, I cut diagonally across Liberty Street and thus eliminated the probability of being seen from the McCalmont house. I also came home from school that first several days, via the alley which paralleled Liberty Street but was behind the houses on the far side of the street from Elou's.

COORDINATION BETWIXT MAN AND BEAST
(Circa 1902)

And then there was the time when I was sluffing along through the snow on my drowsy way home from an uneventful session in Miss Bauman's second grade class. I was on the sidewalk of Fifteenth Street, just south of that, all inclusive alley outlet (Osmers, Grants, McCalmonts and Plummers).

That alley began in a depression just below Sixteenth Street and ended in a precipitous, twelve-foot ramp at Fifteenth Street. This steep end of the alley was bricked and today it was covered with a thin sheet of crystal clear ice. It was a frigid day and the landscape was several inches deep with the customary white covering. Three little preschool girls, with reckless abandon, were alternately pulling a small sled from the street to the top of this icy slide, mounting the sled after packing themselves tightly in place, urging the sled to start by repeatedly umphing their shoulders to the slick down grade of this twelve foot slope and shooting out about ten feet onto the street when the deep snow brought the sled to a quick stop,

Clumping down the street, westward bound[10], came a heavy farm bobsled apparently devised by an ingenious farmer, by removing the wheels from his farm wagon and substituting two heavy sleds. This vehicle was drawn along at a steady pace by a white horse which trotted along at a carefree pace, clump, clump, clump, clump. The driver seemed to be as carefree as the motor. He was a well-aged black man who lolled in the left-hand corner of the board which had been nailed across the bed of the conveyance to serve as a seat.

When I first noticed their approach, the driver was loosely holding the reins in one hand and was apparently sleeping. The three girls had just arrived at the top of the slide, had mounted the sled and were in the process of umphing it into motion. Due to crowded quarters

---

[10] 15th Street runs North and South. More than likely, the wagon was heading southward.

on their sled the front girl sat with her legs extended straight forward, beyond the body of the sled. As they flashed down that steep decline, the farm sledge was just about to cross their line of travel - clump, clump, clump, clump.

I had often heard the expression "His heart jumped into his throat" but, had never before, in my seven or eight years of life had that feeling, until this moment. The horse, pulling that heavy farm sledge, was clumping along at a steady pace, clump, clump, clump, clump. As the girls on the sled streaked down that short incline, they headed for certain disaster. I heard a quiet voice say "whoa." The anti-action was immediate, the horse stopped in his tracks. I could have vouched for the fact that his right front and left rear hooves came to an instantaneous stop while in mid-air. The driver had not moved, had not pulled on the reins, had not shouted, he had merely said "whoa" just once in a voice little higher than a whisper. I even then wondered if he was awake.

The sled stopped midway beneath the sledge. The left leg of the first girl was actually touching the shining curved runner of that back bob. My first impulse, as the girls disentangled themselves and fell off of the sled, weeping, was to drop my second year spelling book and slide down and congratulate that black man. But I was much too timid for such a gesture.

The children regained their feet but all three of them were as white as the snow covered street. What a glorious display of obedience had been registered between this man and his horse! A messy tragedy had been averted as suddenly as it could have occurred.

HURRY HARRY HURRY
(Circa 1903)

And then there was the time when I was sitting at my desk in Miss Eschelman's third grade room with my hands folded, as was my custom, it was the moment before the teacher called the class to order in anticipation of the start of the morning session. The classroom door burst open and Harry, a late arrival, as was his custom, moved silently into the room and stood by his desk. He glanced at me from across the room and with a triumphant smile lighting up his face, proceeded to telegraph to me the good news of the day. He held his right hand above his head with fingers stretched, and alternately clasped his hand and extended his fingers. He did this five consecutive times.

I was astonished, for each of the fingers represented one cent which he had accumulated and was to be shared with me after school. Often he had signaled a nickel, on one memorable occasion a dime, but a whole quarter was almost unbelievable.

My mouth flew open in astonishment and I telegraphed for a repeat of the amount by making a set of eyeglasses with my hands, thumbs to index fingers, and staring at harry through this simulated pair of spectacles. Harry immediately repeated the five fingers five times signal and sat down. Miss Eschelman tapped her pencil violently on her desk and stared quizzically at the bearer, to me, of such glorious news.

A whole quarter! A trip to town was inevitable. How I managed to complete the day's work I'll never know, except possibly for the fact that my last initial "S" was far down the alphabet and Miss Eschelman had not yet learned to surprise students with an occasional call for recitation beginning at the wrong end of the alphabet, thereby finding out how little the Smiths, the Stansburys, the Taylors, and the Williamsons knew about current assignments.

After school, Harry and I swept into town arm in arm. Our first stop was at the Joe Riesenman drug store, where we chose from the candy counter, and to the disgust of the fountain boy. Two of these, two

47

of these, four of these and two of those until we had splurged a nickel. Harry was most unselfish. He invariably divided, with me, all of his purchases. He ignored the clerk's suggestion that we could get five marshmallows for a cent, but five was not easily divided into two portions.

Next, we entered Rollya's merchandise mart with twenty cents still in my buddy's tightly clenched fist. We studied the toy department carefully and at great length. Went back to the sporting goods display, were tempted, but not convinced that we should spend another nickel on a box of BBs, easily divided, but neither of us owned an air gun. We retreated to the curb in front of the store and while sitting there Harry divided the candy and while we ate we mulled over what was to be our next purchase.

A boy walked by, idly swinging a baseball bat. Harry jumped to his feet and shouted to me, "Come on George." We again entered the store where Harry picked up two nickel baseballs, handed one to me and put the other in his own pants pocket. Then he studied the contents of the bat rack, hefting each bat in turn. After a thorough inspection of every bat in the store, Harry finally selected two which suited him and took them to the clerk.

Harry was frustrated, the bats cost a dime apiece. Although the price was disappointing to Harry, I assured him that only one of us would bat at a time. Let's just get one bat, in fact one ball would be sufficient.

My suggestion concerning the bat was accepted by Harry. But he turned thumbs down on the ball theory. He divulged to me, in great detail, how a ball might easily be lost, but seldom a bat.

He walked casually up to Thirteenth Street, turned right to Elk, each of us nurturing a nickel baseball in a pants pocket. Harry was idly swinging the bat at an imaginary ball. It never occurred to me to produce the ball from my pocket and toss it to him for something more substantial to swing at. He turned into Elk Street. There was no traffic here. At Harry's suggestion, I crossed the street to the north side, produced the ball from my pocket and tossed it to the batter who had remained on the south side. Now a nickel baseball is as lifeless as a dead rabbit, being made up of scrap felt tightly compressed and covered by an oil cloth "horse hide" - it just will not bounce. So dutifully I "wound-up" and aimed the ball at Harry who took a tremendous swing at it, and much to our combined astonishment the ball took off, sailed over my head as I leaped to catch it. A crash of glass behind me. I turned around to see what had been broken. The big parlor window of the little house directly behind me had been irreparably smashed.

Nor did I tarry to ponder why that ball should have been so much more active than the customary nickel one. I faded! Crossing the street in zero seconds, I flashed past Harry like he was standing still, which he was not.

Whoosh, up Elk Street towards home I sizzled, not giving Harry more than a frightened glance as I passed him by. Harry regained his reason in a split second and I could hear him clattering up the sidewalk with ever decreasing cadence. I turned to see what was detaining him. The bat, which he was still carrying in both hands, was running a too slow interference for his potential speed. I shouted back to him to drop it, at the same time my cap became dislodged from my head and fell to the ground. Hearing the ping and clatter of the dropped bat and realizing that I had done all that I could for my buddy and writing off my lost cap as a donation to the furtherance of speed, I settled down to putting as much distance as possible between myself and that broken window.

My feet pumped like pistons as that Elk Street sidewalk disappeared beneath them. The curb at Fourteenth Street was hardly noticeable. I glided over it like a startled gazelle in full flight. If there had been an LS&MS[11] train of freight cars blocking my way at that instant I felt that I could have leaped over the biggest box car without interrupting my stride. I was scared, really scared. Fifteenth Street was cleared in like fashion. The sidewalk was gone now from my side of the

---

[11] Lake Shore and Michigan Southern Railway (1869-1914)

street, but the weed grown path offered a direct line towards home and I hoped, sanctuary.

I zipped on. Harry had been lost long ago in my onward rush. Through the cow gate to Mitchell's field and thus into the well kept garden in back of McCalmont's house. I figured later that whatever detective might have been following me, I had presented a perfect clue to my whereabouts. A path as straight as a stretched rubber band, through trampled onions and uprooted tomato plants led to the back gate of McCalmont's iron fence directly opposite our house.

I continued through the gate and across Sixteenth Street at hair raising speed and only slowed to a jog as I rounded the rear of our house and found that one of the two "slide-down" doors had been conveniently left open. I entered and hurried down those seven steps into the cool, dark of the dirt paved cellar, slumped on the bottom step and leaned my head on the top of the open wooden barrel which was about half full of rock salt, an indispensable item in the manufacture of ice cream at our house.

After recuperating from my trip, but still breathing hard, I considered how my happiness had diminished since, just a few hours before, when Harry had first telegraphed to me the acquisition of a whole quarter.

I pondered, "What had we accomplished here?" The quarter was gone. Our bellies were stuffed with caramels and chocolate drops. My cap was gone. Harry's bat was gone. My ball was gone. We had broken someone's parlor window and we were both on the "lam."

Perhaps though that felt stuffed nickel baseball, still reposing, I hoped, in Harry's pants pocket would help compensate us for our losses. Ain't life unpredictable?

LET'S LOOK UNDER THAT ONE
(Circa 1902-1903)

And then there was the time when Carl Read and my big brother P.W. each of whom had accumulated a handful of pennies, hit upon the scheme of startling a few members of the small fry set by demonstrating how money grows under rocks.

The procedure was simple. Approximately twenty five pennies were concealed, as a one and one-half inch stack, in the closed left hand of the "operator." He then strolled through the rock-strewn second clearing conducting a "Let's look under this rock" tour with the small but innocent victim at his side. The operator would approach a cobble stone sized boulder which could be readily dislodged from its earthly bed. He would reach down, upend the rock with his right hand and quickly while the crickets were scampering for cover, transfer the stacked pennies in his left hand to rest between his thumb and forefinger of the right hand. Then, with a lightening move, reach into the depression where the rock had lain and expose the coins to the view and amazement of his awe-struck helper. The money was presumably dropped into a pants pocket but was really again concealed in his left hand in anticipation of the next rock turnover. The stone was always carefully replaced so as to provide a fertile bed for more money to grow. The story being that some rocks would produce money and some would not.

Saint Clair Riesenman, about the same age as P.W., was enthralled with this trick and proposed to go "all out" and improve the illusion by growing silver coins instead of pennies. He procured twenty quarters by raiding the cash register of his father's drug store, where he did spare time work behind the soda fountain.

These twenty quarters made a neat little stack of silver coins, a trifle more than two inches long which was readily concealed in the closed hand. Don't misunderstand me, this five dollar's worth of silver was not swiped, merely borrowed from the register and would be replaced on the following day.

Saint then adopted a victim - me. We set forth on our adventure along the fence row in the cow pasture behind the house. P.W. was not available, he was in the barn constructing a pair of stilts from two bed slats, and beside he had spent most of his stack of pennies on the previous day. Carl Read had not put in an appearance this morning, so Saint and I ventured forth alone.

He found a suitable football sized boulder which he upended and much to my pleasure and amazement, produced a stack of quarters from the spot beneath. In a frenzy of anticipation, I took out on my own, tugging at other stones in the immediate vicinity. I found no money but I carefully replaced each stone on the theory that it might produce silver or copper for a further search.

Saint found another likely looking boulder, called me to come and watch, upended it and I was again bewildered when he lifted out a stack of quarters. But oh what trouble over-confidence may bring! Saint grew careless and must have figured that a really good operator could "salt" his garden. While I was off again frantically turning over stone after stone, he raised another rock, planted the treasure neatly in the dirt and lowered the rock gently back into place. Then he called to me. I was diligently tugging at a boulder which was too large for my strength and Saint came over and helped me raise it - but alas, no money.

Then it happened. Silently - from nowhere - Katy Read appeared at our side. She had come down from her house, seeking me to play school in our cobweb filled class room under the front porch. Due to Saint's and my concentration on the money search, neither of us saw her approach our mining operations. She appeared like a phantom while Saint was helping me with the big stone and the first glimpse we got of her, she was bending over and pulling hard on the rock under which Saint had placed the twenty quarters. She pulled the rock loose and quickly grabbed the money from its resting spot - shouted hilariously - dropped the treasure into her pinafore pocket and eagerly continued her search for more rocks to upend. I noticed that she had not completed her chore by failing to replace the rock and I shouted to her to put it back so that it might grow more money. Saint was "beside himself" with dismay. I innocently continued my search, now urged to even greater effort by seeing the results of Katy's beginner's luck. Saint tried unsuccessfully to recover his loss by forcing a laugh and explaining to Katy that those quarters were really his and that he had, just a moment before, put them under the rock for the purpose of fooling me.

Katy was unbelieving and adamant and threatened to run home and tell her mother that he (Saint) was trying to steal what was rightfully hers. Saint appealed to me. I was Katy's good friend. Wouldn't I try to convince her that the whole operation was a hoax and that the money really belonged to him?

Poor saint, he had three problems forced upon him all at once. First and possibly the most insurmountable, he must enlighten and disillusion me and make me understand that what had been purported to be "money farming" was really only a trick. This in itself was like trying to convince me that Santa Claus was a simple myth, and untrue legend. Second, he had to prevail upon me, as Katy's trusted friend and cohort, to plead with her for the return of the silver. And third, that all of this must be accomplished as speedily as possible, to insure the culmination of the project before Katy took flight with the twenty quarters.

Although Saint's disclosure to me that the entire operation was a farce and it had a valid, reasonable flavor, I remained stupidly unconvinced that the money had not grown under the rock. But sensing the distress in his plea, I suggested to Katy that we were a team, all our findings should be equally divided except that Saint, who was head scout and master of the hunt was deserving of a larger share.

This argument fell on deaf ears as far as Katy was concerned. I scarcely believed it myself, for had I not seen him pocket, for his own advantage the silver which had grown under the first two rocks? Saint added a few words of his own to the discussion and finally Katy searched out of her pinafore pocket, two quarters which she gave to Saint, and a third one she presented to me.

Then with an "I have to go now" she ran like the wind up the rock strewn hill towards home with four dollars and twenty five cents of the John Riesenman drug store operating capital clinking in her pocket.

Saint turned and walked dejectedly to his house.

"And what did you do George?" Oh, me? I furiously resumed my search under promising rocks until my mother called me home for lunch.

AND AGAIN IT WAS DENNY
(Circa 1902-1903)

And then there was the time when my Brother Bert and I were performing on the pipe fence which our Dad had erected at the base of our front terrace. We were turning somersaults, hanging by our knees and even attempting to tight rope walk on that sturdy pipe.

"Oh, oh, look at here!" exclaims Bert, reaching down and picking up a nickel from the grass, worn thin by many an acrobatic foot, for that pipe served as the neighborhood gymnasts' horizontal bar. Immediately we both searched for more treasures along that rail, and lucky me - I came up with two pennies at about the same place beneath the pipe were Bert had found the nickel. This fortune had undoubtedly fallen from the pockets of one of our athletic friends while he was turning a somersault on that good old pipe.

Determined to find the one who have lost the seven cents and possibly returning it to him, we went through the whole catalog of friends who had recently performed on our bar. Ralph Evans and Victor Bigler had been in our front yard when we had been called to lunch just an hour ago. Ralph was immediately eliminated from suspicion because we knew Ralph never had any money. It must have been Victor. But then a happy thought struck me - Victor's mother always made his pants, and without pockets for the sake of economizing on material and as a labor saver. Grandma Read, according to Bobby, had learned this trick down in Clearfield and had passed it along to Mrs. Bigler. Victor also always wore a turtleneck sweater and that fact did away with the possibility of loss of funds from a shirt pocket. Sure he kept his handkerchief, if any, in a fold of the sweater, but no money.

Bert and I conferred and he promoted, what I thought at the time, was a very clever idea, although it reminded me of a former project of his wherein he and I were both to remove our shoes at the designated spot in our lawn, after having played in the Evans' sand pile. We were then to pour the accumulated sand from our shoes into that one spot. He

55

reasoned that eventually we too would have a sand pile. After a few days of diligently following this routine we lost our unloading point and discontinued the practice.

But now to the new promotion which Bert had devised. I was to act as the "shill" and clumsily attempt to have to get up on the pipeline when I saw a playmate approaching, especially if his pockets jingled - this, of course, would exclude Ralph and Victor - but we have many other gymnastic and gullible friends. My vain attempts to mount the bar should properly cause the new arrival to stop, look and then inquire, "What the devil are you trying to do Jimmy?" Then following accepted shill routine, I would explain that I was trying to get on the pipe and hang by my knees and that only a very few of my friends had ever accomplished this particular feat.

Presto! The new comer would promptly go into action and sit on that horizontal pipe, slide over backwards and hang by his knees. This maneuver was intended to promptly disgorge his pockets of most of the jingling contents and if it was not apparent to the "customer" these coins would be gathered up by my brother while I moved down to the far end of the fence and urged the athlete to show me how he did it, exclaiming some set phrase such as "Gosh, that was great," or "Gee, you're pretty good."

The sophisticated Dennison Grant happened by at this juncture, walking stiffly as was Denny's custom. I thought that I detected the jingle of silver so I promptly went into my bit, awkwardly attempting to pull myself up to a sitting position on the bar. Denny stopped, looked and finally propounded the required question, leaving out, quite naturally, any reference to Satan. My answer followed the accepted form, "Trying to hang by my knees," and "Only a few fellows can do it."

From this point on, the routine varied from the expected course. Denny removed his big, checkered yachting cap, handed it to me and ordered, "Here hold." I accepted the cap and was about to place it on the grass beside me. Denny motioned to me and pointed to the cap and again ordered, "Hold!"

I dutifully complied. He then removed from one of his knickers' pockets, two quarters, a dime and a neatly folded one dollar bill. These he placed in the cap which I extended toward him. He searched the second pants pocket and produced a handful of coins which he also dumped into the cap. Then, with unexpected agility, he mounted the bar, swung down backwards and hung from his knees. I detected a smirk of disdain in the look of superiority he now foisted on me. He dropped gracefully to his feet, accepted the cap full of money (I had never seen so much in one pile) and without a word, strutted stiff legged back in the direction of his home.

I could, of course, have grabbed a bit of loose change from the cap while Denny was performing and thereby accomplished the designed purpose of a shill, but the thought never occurred to me. And so Bert and I abandoned the entire technique, deciding the even if the loot had to be picked up from the ground it did border on larceny.

ANOTHER "SHORTY" EPISODE
(Circa 1902-1903)

And then there was the time when four of us boys had just completed an inspection of the new construction work on Osmer's corn crib. We, of course, waited until the carpenters had finished for the day and then, after walking, crawling in, over, under, around and through the partially completed crib we departed, each of us carrying a "borrowed" eight foot scantling[12].

And brother Bert's suggestion we stood these four pieces of two by two lumber in the ground in the field directly behind the Read house. These four uprights made the corner posts of a structure about the size of a compact phone booth. Newspaper was acquired from Bobby Read's chicken house and was spread out and tacked to the scantlings on three sides, making, in essence, a rather lopsided little house with paper siding. The purpose of the house was to provide a realistic blaze for the "squirt gun" fire brigade to extinguish.

A squirt gun was a handmade item, fashioned from a joint of bamboo, opened at one end and with a hole about the size of a small nail drilled or punched into the closed end. A stick, slightly larger in diameter than a pencil, and about 3 inches longer than the section of bamboo, was wrapped with a piece of cloth at one end and tied with a piece of string, much like a bandaged[13] finger. This was the piston, or plunger, and when soaked with water and pushed bandage end first, into the open end of the bamboo, the whole made a very affective water gun. The gun could be loaded by submerging the nozzle end into a bucket of water and cocked by withdrawing the plunger to its outside limit and be discharged by pushing the plunger forcefully into the barrel of the gun.

---

[12] A timber of relatively slight width and thickness, as a stud or rafter in a house frame.

[13] The modern adhesive bandage was not invented until 1920.

The newspaper siding was set on fire and the four of us, with much whooping and hollering, quickly extinguished the blaze with our squirt guns.

The shouting apparently attracted the attention of Shorty Evans, who appeared on the scene just as the last of the burning paper had been subdued. Shorty took stock of the situation and proposed that we put on a really gala demonstration. We were to strengthen the structure with a few cross beams so that a board could be laid flat inside the house about four feet off the ground. Shorty would perch himself on this crosspiece and at the proper instant, would leap to safety from, presumably, the second floor of the house through a simulated window in the paper, just in time to avoid being consumed by the raging flames. At Shorty's insistence, the house was moved about twenty feet, to a more advantageous position near a large butternut tree. A log was rolled up near the front of the house and was to serve as the front row seats for the spectators.

As this superb spectacle demanded that everything be precisely to Shorty's liking, the grand conflagration was delayed until the following morning. This postponement gave us an opportunity to make the required changes in the structure, advertise the forthcoming event throughout the neighborhood and appoint the principals. Bert was elected the fire department's battalion chief, for was it not Bert's bamboo fishing pole which had been sawed up to make those squirt guns? "Grinny" and Bobby Read were to be the "pump men" and Eddie Riesenman was assigned to be the water supply administrator, he was to accompany the firefighters and carry the bucket of water for charging their guns. Ralph Evans, Shorty's little brother, would sound the alarm by beating on a piece of iron pipe with a railroad spike.

The house was moved and reconstructed to fulfill Shorty's plan and the outline of a window was smeared, with paint, on the newspaper at the front. In order to make the conflagration more realistic, a great quantity of paper was crumpled and scattered on the ground floor of the house. This would, according to Shorty, create a sizable blaze and add to the splendor and excitement of this massive spectacular.

In the morning, we gathered at the scene. Front row, log seats, were given to the first of the spectators to arrive. Katy Read, Dorothy Evans, Anna Riesenman, Eddie's big sister, who had to come to find out what her little brother meant by "supply minister" as he had explained that was his title. Harry Henderson was there, as were Victor Bigler and two little kids from elk street, who were recipients of some of our oral advertising propaganda.

Shorty was very busy inspecting and supervising, walking around the "properties" with his thumbs in his belt. After ordering Ralph to collect a couple of pieces of old tar paper from the Evans backyard and adding them to the crumpled newspaper inside the house to, as Shorty said, "make good black smoke." He ordered the fire brigade to deploy behind some bushes about twenty yards behind the spectators.

Shorty then disappeared into the paper house through the open back, he punched a hole through the painted window and waved confidently to the breathless front row crowd. Ralph was over anxious, jumped the cue and began to beat furiously on the iron pipe.

Here came the department! Bert, followed by "Grinny" and Bobby, all three with squirt guns loaded and cocked. Then came Eddie, his empty bucket clattering at his heels. In the tenseness and excitement of the moment, he had completely forgotten to fill his bucket at the spring.

Shorty's face appeared at the punctured window and he scowled at his little brother for sounding the alarm prematurely. He shouted, at the top of his lungs, "What's a matter of you Ralph? I ain't even lit it yet."

Then a wisp of smoke a rose from the doomed structure and almost immediately, as the crumpled paper burst into flames, the house was a blazing inferno. Shouts from the spectators urged Shorty to jump - jump. But Shorty did not jump. The paper siding at the front of the house curled and turned black and the pieces of char swirled up in the rising air currents. Meanwhile the over-anxious department had exhausted their loaded guns and were desperately pumping them in the "Supply Minister's" empty bucket in a vain attempt to reload. The chief ordered Eddie to hurry to the spring and fill his bucket and then, with a stick, the chief prodded around in the blazing tar paper in search of who knew what.

The girls shrieked, Ralph ran home, Eddie started to follow orders and then dropped his empty bucket and disappeared into the bushes. Dorothy, Shorty's sister became hysterical, screamed and cried. At last, when the fire had subsided, and the only vestiges of it that remained were a few pieces of smoking tar paper, and Dorothy's screams had reached a high crescendo, Shorty calmly appeared from behind the butternut tree, smiling triumphantly. He had perpetrated a hoax on the whole assembly, spectators, bell ringer and fire department alike.

He managed to lead Dorothy home, although she was still in shock, shrieking, blubbering and weeping and occasionally giving vent to the scream of "Oh they've killed my brother."

I was told that Shorty was confined to his room for three days - not because he had frightened his sister, not because he had played with matches but because he had sneaked out of the house that morning without washing the breakfast dishes.

BUT MAYBE YOU WEREN'T ACQUAINTED WITH EMILY
(Circa 1902-1903)

And then there was the time that John Berlin and my brother Bert were squatted in the Berlin's front yard, engaged, half-heartedly, in a game of mumblety-peg.[14] The afternoon was hot and sultry. John's sister had tired of attempting to build railway tunnels in the skimpy little pile of very dry sand. The tunnels kept collapsing. This inspired Emily to sneak into the kitchen and procure a pail of water with which to moisten the sand. When she returned with a full bucket she tripped on a stump at the sand pile, the water missed the sand but made a delightful, sloppy goo of an expanse of brown dust on the outskirts of the sand.

The goo was pleasantly cool to the touch and the manufacture of mud balls immediately resulted. We built up quite a supply: small round ones, medium sized, flat ones and very large, very crude ones. Our stock of raw material was soon depleted and Em suggested that we might throw the balls at the wasps' nest which was most cleverly concealed above the front screen door of the Berlin residence. We succeeded in thoroughly aggravating the wasps and defacing the front of the house with mud. Then a shot by Emily was really accurate, it hit the nest squarely and caused a real disturbance among its residents. One reconnoitering wasp investigated the progress of the mumblety-peg game, kissed John in a most unfriendly manner and thereby caused cessation of both the game and the bombardment.

John was furious and immediately blamed his little sister and me for the outrage perpetrated against his dignity and his bottom. He cautiously refrained from making a public issue of his anger (his mother had instructed him concerning his inclination to pick on sister). This wasp's action, however broke our foursome up into two rival camps,

---

[14] A game in which the players try to flip a knife from various positions so that the blade will stick into the ground.

62

friendly but rival. John, unable to wreak his resentment on his little sister concluded that I (the smallest male of the group) was in collusion with Em, and promptly accused me of urging the wasp to sting him. Big brother Bert, John's equal in age and physical ability, came to my defense and argued that no one of us was more to blame than another and the incident was wholly one of chance and of the wasp's preference. John was wearing short thin pants with two large holes which were direly in need of patches. Because of Bert's intervention, the four of us again became amicable and began a search for a diversion, pleasurable but less hazardous than wasp bombing.

Athletics were suggested and we took turns at chinning ourselves on the porch railing. Emily outdid us all in this activity. So John suggested the standing broad jump. In this too, Emily out jumped us all and John placed a miserable fourth. John again became incensed due to the fact that both his sister and I had beaten him and suggested the old standby, a foot race.

We lined up in the middle of Sixteenth Street, facing down towards our house and as John and Bert were older than Em and me they insisted that we be given a handicap of five paces. The finish line was indefinite but we understood it to be about opposite Tilly Bridges front gate. John called the start of the race with the customary, one for the money, two for the show chant. At the word GO, Em and I tore down the middle of the street, side by side, and with the grim determination that the ten foot lead which we had was going to be maintained. As we passed the Allen's house, we had not been overtaken. We gritted our teeth and forced ourselves to even greater effort as we went by Victor Bigler's house in a cloud of dust. At Bridges' corner gatepost I couldn't resist a look over my shoulder - Em and I were still traveling at top speed, neck and neck, down that steep Sixteenth Street grade. We were alone in the race! I shouted my surprising discovery to Em and we slithered to a stop. Away in the distance, in the direction from which we had come, we saw our opposition - those two scheming boys, still running pell mell[15] away from us, and now well into Miller Park.

Em and I walked slowly back up the road. We considered ourselves the winners and it didn't immediately occur to me that Bert and John had maliciously ditched us. But Em, being more worldly wise than myself, must have suspected their dastardly motive, for just then Mrs. Berlin appeared on her front porch and shouted, "Emill-l-e-e - young lady did you put all of this mud on the porch?"

"No mam," simpered Emily, "John did it and then ran away."

"Drat that ungrateful boy," whined Mrs. Berlin, "Just wait 'till I get my hands on him,"

Emily murmured, "Yes'm" and smiled at me. Our chagrin would soon be avenged.

"Em," says I , "Why did you lie to your mother?"

"Oh," says Em, grinning in pleasurable anticipation, "John would have done as much for me."

---

[15] In a confused, rushed, or disorderly manner.

CHAGRIN
(Circa 1902-1903)

---- True incident as reported, in the third person, by the victim himself. ----

And then there was the time when George Allen was standing in front of the Joe Riesenman drug store, looking wistfully thru the big plate glass window at the soda fountain, where luscious cold concoctions were being served to customers by the man in the white apron. The afternoon was hot and humid. George stood there wiping his sweaty brow with the, already sopping, sleeve of his pink and white striped shirt.

In the center of the marble topped fountain rested a square pedestal. The pedestal sported a tall, clear glass dome in which was mounted a small figurine resembling either a fairy princess or a sea nymph. From the top of the head of this figure a very fine stream of water was projected against the rounded top of the dome and then cascaded and rippled down the inside of this glass enclosure. The little stream of water made a hissing sound when it hit the inside of the dome. This hiss was constant and was very pleasing to hear, especially in the hot store and the shimmer of the falling water added an air of coolness to the scene.

Jauntily attired Ned Grant emerged from the store, paused at George's side and said, "Hot isn't it George?"

"Yes it is Mr. Grant, I'm about to burn up," replied George.

"How'd you like a cold drink?" inquired Ned.

"I'd like that very much," says George.

"Well you go inside and tell Fred to give you a Boston float and charge it to me," says Ned, "I've got an appointment over at the Exchange Bank or I'd go with you."

After a quick, "Thank you, Mr. Grant," George entered the store and perched himself on one of the wire stools at the fountain. Fred, the young man in the white apron was wiping off the counter with a dirty towel.

"What'll it be?" he asked of George. Hesitatingly, George replied that he would like a Boston Float and would he please charge it to Mr. Grant.

Fred concealed a grin, picked up an empty glass, plunked it into one of the silvery holders, bent low behind the fountain and waving an ice-cream scoop in his free hand he banged the metal covers of the various freezer tanks, one after another, presaging a delightful concoction, redundant with four or more scoops of ice-cream of various flavors. Finally he straightened up to his full height, filled the still empty glass with tepid water from the tap and slid it, complete with it's metal holder across the marble top of the counter where it came to rest directly in front of our hero. Then Fred fumbled with an open box of crackers, produced a small round soda cracker and adroitly flipped it on top of the water in the glass.

Turning away from the counter and ringing up NO SALE on the cash register, Fred murmured in a voice which was audible to the five or six other fountain customers, "One Boston Float and charge it to Mr. Grant." The other soda fountain patrons turned, as a unit, to stare at the perspiring boy whose taste in cooling beverages was so strange.

George sheepishly slid off of the stool and rushed blindly from the store. He confessed to me that, for a number of years following the episode of the Boston Float, he cringed every time he heard the sound of the stream from a garden hose being used to wash a side walk or the sound of a locomotive with its cylinder bleeder valves open. He maintained that the hiss of these operations reminded him all too poignantly of the most embarrassing moment of his youth.

THE CIDER LADY
(Circa 1902-1903)

And then there was the time when George Berlin and I were sitting under that Russet apple tree in his front yard, casually sampling the few apples which had fallen from the tree after they had become a bit riper than was necessary for good eating. We were not permitted to climb that particular tree and I expressed my distaste for those squashy, partially rotted apples. George, on the other hand, professed a definite liking for them, claiming that he was very fond of apple cider, and since cider was not immediately available, those semi-rotten apples were a first rate substitute.

The difference of opinion waxed into quite an argument and grew louder by the minute. George upholding the case for the brown, squashy, over-ripe fruit and I defending my right to dislike them. George and I were working up to the point of exchanging blows on behalf of our separate views on rotten apples when John, George's elder brother, came out of the house and joined in the discussion. "Youse guys are arging about nuttin," volunteered John. "And Georgie if you want cider I know where there's a lady what keeps a apple orchid and she makes so much cider she gives it away to anyone what asks fer it."

"Where she?" inquired George."

"Oh," says John, thinking fast, "She lives out a piece on Grassy Road." Then, overcoming his temporary confusion at having to pinpoint the exact location, John continued boastfully, "I kin show you where she's at if you don't mind a short walk."

"Who she?" queried George.

"Name's Mrs. Betsiross." replies John after some hesitation.

John was generally reliable, but had an inherent aptitude for exaggeration and neither George nor I had the slightest suspicion of John's lack of veracity, so the story of the "Cider Lady" being completely a John Berlin fairy tale scarcely entered our minds.

67

George disappeared into the house to procure a two-quart tin pail, and I hurried home to inform my mother that I was going to walk out Grassy Road with John and George Berlin, for a short distance. I picked up a Mason jar on my way out of the kitchen, (nothing like going prepared). My brother Bert and Don Allen joined us under the Russet apple tree, and as they had nothing more interesting to do, they decided to accompany us, and we five started out, with John as our fearless guide.

No use to go the length of Sixteenth Street to get to Elk Street, which was the townward extension of Grassy Road. At John's command we cut diagonally across the first clearing, past the Arch Osmer house and approached Grassy Road at an angle. This resulted in no hardship except that I clumsily smashed my Mason jar while negotiating the Osmer garden fence. We jumped down off the stone wall which kept Arch Osmer's front yard from sliding onto Grassy Road and we proceeded west at a brisk rate, following after John.

After about a quarter mile of very dusty walking, the five of us, again at John's "suggestion," left the dirt and took to the LS & MS tracks, which ran parallel to the road. We attempted to walk a rail, follow the leader style. John, who was barefooted, of course led the way. And George, also without foot covering, followed. The rail was burning hot. I could feel it through the leather soles of my shoes, and I wondered how John and George could stand it in their bare feet.

George, finally, but too late, gave in to better judgment and walked the ties. He began to whine, and his whimpering influenced John to revert to the road and we continued on for another half mile or so.

We overtook a steam tractor going in our direction and dragged along beside it for some little distance. We referred to it as a "thrashing machine." It was a self-propelled power plant, designed to be belted to a thresher, it's prime purpose for existence. This "thrashing machine" had to make frequent stops as it traveled the roadway, for it's boiler capacity was apparently not sufficient to keep up the pace.

A crew of two men, an engineer and a fireman, was in charge of this smoking monster. We exchanged pleasantries with these two

68

operators and learned that the engineman's name was Trilby and the coal shoveler's was Bruce. Finally, at one of the frequent stops for lack of steam, we bid Trilby and Bruce goodbye and continued our trek in search of the "Cider Lady." On and on we walked. We passed the water pumping station on French Creek and the road soon became two wagon ruts. I (for one) had never been out this far before. We plodded on, John constantly assuring us that it was just a little bit "further."

We came to a farm house with apple trees in the front yard and were all confident that this, finally, was the "Cider Lady's" home. But John said "Nope this ain't it, it's just a little further." A sun tanned woman appeared at the farm house gate, inquired where we were bound, offered us some apples and tried to soothe George's blistered feet by having him soak them in his little pail, which she had filled with cool water from the pump. George was again whimpering. John asked the lady her name. She said "Mrs. Allen," which brought John to the front, questioning her as to the possibility of establishing a relationship with himself. He lost interest when Mrs. Allen's black husband and three little black children appeared on the front porch. We noted, for the first time, that what we had mistaken for suntan was obviously the natural skin of a light colored negro.

Our little troupe pushed on, John constantly insisting that we were almost there and repeatedly telling us that he was familiar with the surroundings and "it's just a little bit further." Finally John called a halt to our travels, gathered us around him and made an announcement. "Fellas," he blurted out, "we're lost!" Doom had overtaken us! I started to cry, joining George, who had scarcely ceased his whimpering since burning his feet on that railroad rail.

I pictured us starving to death out in this great nowhere land and I feverishly clutched the two apples which I had obtained from Mrs. Allen and concealed in my blouse, determined to keep from a death by starvation for as long as possible.

More mature heads, however, prevailed. Bert took over the leadership from John by assuring us that we were not lost - all we had to do was reverse our direction and we could follow Grassy Road back to Sixteenth Street. Or failing that, revert to the railroad tracks and follow them right into Fourteenth Street. We were all tired by now but the possibility of being overtaken by dusk urged us to hasten along those two wagon tracks. We were now traveling in the direction of home.

Soon we passed the point where the ruts converged with the dust of Grassy Road, then we passed the pumping station, George keeping up a constant whine due to his burned feet. John remonstrated with him, calling him a sissy and adding, "Ain't ya got no gumption? My feet burns too."

We plodded on, sometimes breaking into a frenzied trot at Bert's insistence. Soon we came upon the "thrashing machine" - now pulled to the side of the road with fires banked.[16] Trilby was asleep on the deck behind the steering wheel and Bruce was perched on top of one of the two enormous driving wheels, busily engaged in consuming a bread and jelly sandwich. They apparently had decided to call it a day. We greeted Bruce cordially and in reply he held up a silencing finger, cautioning us not to wake his engineer.

Two empty pint whiskey bottles were lying on the iron floor at Trilby's side and another one, only half empty, was clutched in his grimy hand. And as Don Allen aptly stated, "Ya couldn't wake him up with a brass bad."

Ploughing on, saying little, we were all a bit anxious to get home before nightfall. Then, we saw in the distance approaching us my Father and Mother accompanied by my elder brother P. W. and a woman whom I didn't immediately recognize. It was Don's maiden aunt as I gathered from the excited pitch of her voice and her opening remark upon first sighting us. "More'n proble all those boys could do with a good hot bath." We must indeed have presented a disreputable sight, five hot, tired, dirty, dust encrusted urchins struggling along that inappropriately

---

[16] A process to keep the fire going, by allowing the logs/coal to burn down, raking the coals forward in the fire box, then adding logs/coal behind the coals.

named Grassy Road, almost exhausted from an unduly long walk and fearful of not reaching home before dark.

This party, we learned, was a rescue team, which had come at my mother's behest to keep us from starvation and to lead us safely home. Boy! Were we glad to see them! My mother carried a large, brown paper sack containing more apples and many hastily prepared sandwiches. The apples got a cold reception from us, but John gulped down sandwich after sandwich. Gosh! Didn't his family ever feed him?

Now jubilant at being nearly home, we broke into animated conversation. John boastfully explained to my parents, Anna Myer and P.W. that, if it hadn't been for his brother's whining, we would have easily made it to the Cider Lady's farm and returned hours ago. Don poo-pooed this statement of John's and flatly accused him of leading us on a blind chase. "There aid doe Cider Lady dow was they?" goaded Don. Bert and I, secure in the knowledge that we were now almost safely home, joined in accusing John of perfidy. So John, in the presence of the grown folks, gave up trying to lie and admitted, with a forced laugh, that the whole Cider Lady story was a figment of his vivid imagination and that we were stupid to fall for it. Which we undoubtedly were.

JUST A PANSY
(Circa 1902-1903)

And then there was the time when Bert and I were out in the front yard. I was catering to the wants of my yellow pansy, for which I had, just yesterday, plunked down a nickel at Bell's greenhouse. Bert had that heavy garden hose and was, from the top of the front terrace, trying to make its stream reach to the newly planted maple trees just beyond the side walk.

Then along came the smug and dapper Mr. Barnes on his way home to lunch. He was dressed to the gills in an "almost zoot" suit and his little black derby was perched well back on his round head. I first realized that he was passing when I heard him call out to Bert, "Hey kid, watch what you are doing with that hose, you almost splashed me." Neither Bert nor I had any special affection for Mr. Barnes, because of his general demeanor, I suppose.

Bert didn't appreciate being called "kid" but he kept his cool and replied, "Oh Mr. Barnes it never got near you."

"Yes it did," says Barnzie, "you're just a spoiled little brat."

I guess the "brat" turned Bert on, for he calmly raised the trajectory of the stream from that garden hose and soaked Mr. Barnes full in the vest, nor did he lower his aim until Barnes had reasoned that the price of valor, in this instance, was too great and he retreated out of range - the little black derby falling to the pavement, although soaked, was quickly retrieved.

There were no repercussions from the soaking encounter, although I do believe that Mr. Barnes' luncheon tour was, for a few weeks, extended about two blocks. For I observed him, on several occasions, approaching home by way of Elk Street instead of Liberty, thereby making a "scairdy-cat" but sensible detour around our front lawn.

I can still remember my valiant brother standing there impassively, holding that stream of water directly on Mr. Barnes'

72

midriff - there was no attempt made to drop the hose and run. No indecision, no laugh, no sneer from Bert. He just stood there without a change of expression, holding the hose on Barnzie, who first turned red and then livid as he snatched up his hat and departed.

JUST A FLEETING MEMORY
(Circa 1902-1903)

And then there was the time when an elaborate slot machine had been installed in the Joe Riesenman drug store. I say elaborate because it was just that: an ice boxed sized console with an automatic music box - one of the kind that played from a large perforated metal disc and filled the store with heavenly march music whenever a nickel was dropped into its glass enclosed and mirrored innards. In an arc above this glass panel were five round bullseyes, ranging from a white one on the extreme left and proceeded through yellow, green, blue, to red on the right.

The mechanism which revolved the disc was activated by a spring which was wound periodically with a crank at the rear of the box and the power which produced the light behind the various colored glass bullseyes must have been by storage battery for, as I recall, there was no electric plant in our little town, at that time, for home or commercial lighting. We did have electric arc lights placed at strategic street intersections but other than these the town was lighted by natural gas.

When a nickel was pushed into the slot on the machine, the glass panel would light up like a stage, the music would play and one of the five colored bullseyes would gleam. Simultaneously, a small rectangular check would drop into a receptacle attached to the side of the console. The checks were stamped with a value of five, ten, fifteen, twenty or twenty-five cents. If the white light responded to the dropped nickel (as it customarily did) a five cent check would be released, yellow, a ten cent check etc. all the way up to the red light when a twenty-five cent check could be picked up from the receptacle. These checks were good for trade in the store at face value. I heard of one person, Dave Osborn, who had achieved the almost impossible feat of lighting the red light and thereby receiving a quarter's worth of purchases for just one nickel.

On this momentous day, Bert and I each had a nickel to invest. After being assured that I could not possibly lose my nickel, I was induced to reach up and push it into the slot. The lights lighted on stage, the music played and caused me to draw back in excitement. The white bullseye lighted up and I was urged to reach into the pocket and get my five-cent chit. [17] An item which I had completely forgotten in my agitation and excitement at being responsible for those bright lights and that resounding music.

When the music subsided, Bert pushed his nickel into the slot without hesitation. The stage lights came on, the music began and, glory be, the green bullseye lighted and Bert had a fifteen cent purchase check. I was astonished and happy at his good fortune and immediately started to prospect on what we would buy with this unexpected wealth. There were licorice buttons, coltsfoot [18] rock candy, jaw breakers, Smith Brother's cough drops, licorice root, Ju-Ju-Bees and those white sugar-ball candies with a toasted hazelnut inside. I had immediately cashed my five-cent check for a small bag of salted peanuts which I graciously shared with Bert.

He might buy chocolate sodas, one for me and one for himself, at five cents apiece, then there would be a nickel left, for, perhaps, a little pasteboard box of green, gum candy mint leaves. I wouldn't have felt neglected if he had ordered an ice-cream soda for himself at ten cents and let me suffer along with the regular five cent (no ice-cream) concoction.

I followed Bert around the store, from counter to counter like a hungry puppy. Made numerous suggestions at the candy counter and offered my bag of peanuts to him many, many times. All to no avail. He clutched that fifteen cent check in his sweaty fist and finally walked out

---

[17] Chit: a short official note, memorandum, or voucher, typically recording a sum owed.

[18] Coltsfoot is a perennial herbaceous plant used in herbal medicine and has been consumed as a food product with some confectionery products,

to the street with an extremely disappointed little brother still clinging to his reluctant arm.

It was my understanding that this fabulous music box slot machine did not have a very propitious engagement in that drug store. Customers complained about the loudness of the music (I thought it was great). On occasion the light would light and no check would be forthcoming, (causing more complaints) but the culmination of it's life in the Joe Riesenman drug store came the day when a couple of boys had succeeded in attaining the almost impossible red light and were rewarded with a deluge of checks from the twenty-five cent storage compartment. I heard that the boys jostled the machine at the precise moment when the red light lighted.

Mechanical devices in those days were not perfect either.

I THINK YOU WIND IT WITH A KEY
(Circa 1902-1903)

And then there was the time when one Tuesday afternoon, we kids were looking for some productive entertainment and walked over to Miller's pond with the idea of finding out if any of the three or four pond lilies had bloomed since Saturday and were thus good for picking.

Miller's pond was an artificial puddle located centrally on the Miller Estate for the purpose of adding beauty and prestige to the surroundings. It was a twenty by twenty foot pool enclosed on three sides by well kept grass terraces. As this pool was built into the natural slope of the terrain, the lower side was retained by a stone dam, the top of which was made up of granite slabs about a foot wide over which the water from the pond could flow in wet weather and form a very picturesque water fall.

This pool was spring fed from the hillside and the water going over this top slab of the dam was customarily little more than a trickle. Green moss and algae had formed on this "stone bridge" across the pool and the footing was most precarious. Shorty Evans, who was generally barefooted, except when dressed for church or on his way to take clarinet lessons, ventured out onto this slippery crossing and, as a matter of course, dared my brother Bert to follow. Bert, who was wearing laced shoes, stockings and knickers was reluctant to accept the challenge. As I assumed that the dare had been rejected, Ralph, Shorty's little brother and I went down onto the rustic bridge which paralleled the dam and we lay down on the bridge flooring to get a close-up view of the tadpoles and minnows which were cavorting in the six-inch-deep second level pool below the dam.

The bridge on which Ralph and I were lying was a one track crossing for the narrow roadway which wound up and around the beautifully kept hillside below the pond and was built only about four feet from the dam itself and about two feet above the lower pool into which Ralph and I were intently staring. Suddenly, from above our

77

heads we heard a shout of "WATCH OUT!" It was Shorty's voice, he had apparently slid and waded his way safely across that moss covered dam. We looked up to see whom he was warning - there was a splash and looking at us at eye level across that little pool was Bert. He must have finally accepted the dare but was unsuccessful in making the crossing. Fortunately, he landed feet first, a startled but undefeated brother. He didn't even fall down after that eight-foot sudden descent. Only his shoes and stockings were soaked.

He walked (waded) carefully out of that shallow pool, testing for broken bones. Then he sat on the roadway at the end of the bridge and began to unlace his shoes.

"Wot ya wanna do that fer?" called Shorty, from above. "Take them shoes off when there're wet and they'll wrinkle so's you'll never get 'em on agin."

Bert, Ralph, Shorty, Bobby and Katy Read, Dorothy Evans and I conferred and agreed that Bert's shoes should be allowed to dry by keeping them on and walking. We walked down that one track, winding road to the place where it joined the brick pavement. I think it was the alley just beyond Buffalo Street.

"Looky there!" shouted Bobby. And there, making it's way up the alley, was a big square box mounted on four wheels. It was an automobile - the very first that I had ever seen.

As this strange, horseless, contraption left the alley and entered the park on that long, winding road which we had just traversed, we, the whole troop, were astonished and mystified. This "box" made it's way up the steep grade, gears grinding, huffing and puffing like an exhausted runner, we could see a man seated stiffly at the front of the box holding grimly to a wheel on an upright post. He reminded me of the little cast-iron fireman who sat insecurely on the cast-iron front seat of my cast-iron toy hook-and-ladder and was presumably driving the two galloping cast-iron horses. The man on the box wore a billed leather cap and was dressed, not in red enamel, as was his prototype, that little cast-iron fireman, but in a uniform which I later learned was termed livery. He looked like a store window mannequin

When this monstrosity drew along side of our gang, who were now shouting encouragement to the man at the front, he looked anxious and affronted and visibly turned red. He was apparently fearful that the steel spring, which was undoubtedly turning the wheels, would run down before he was able to outdistance us as we ran alongside this weird contraption, shouting and hallooing words of praise for his undertaking. We had no difficulty in keeping pace with this mechanical marvel while it was grinding and groaning up that long, steep road. But the driver became more rigid and his red face turned to a vivid crimson. He probably mistook our words of acclaim for derisive insults. It finally reached the level roadway at which point the robot behind the wheel grabbed one of the levers at his side. A sound similar to the clattering of a stick pulled rapidly across the face of a picket fence came from somewhere inside that rolling box. It lurched forward and soon outdistanced our shouting mob.

This whirring wonder gained speed and soon disappeared in a cloud of dust. It occurred to me that it resembled a miniature Moffat livery stable station bus, rear door and all. It has just come to me, that but for the chain of events leading up to the discovery of this, my first glimpse of an automobile, that this sight might have been delayed for a year and a half or until Mr. McCalmont bought and parked his St. Louis[19] runabout on the street in front of his house.

What chain? You inquire. Well first, our desire to look for waterlily blossoms, then Shorty's dare to Bert to cross the dam, then Bert's soaked shoes and the conclusion which was reached that the wet shoes must be kept on and worn for a long walk to prevent them from shrinking. That box type automobile, although it must have been kept in the immediate neighborhood, was never again seen by me. My! What a thrill I got that day!

---

[19] St. Louis Motor Carriage produced automobiles from 1899 to 1907.

I DIDN'T CARE FOR CIDER NO MORE NO HOW
(Circa 1902-1903)

And then there was the time when I was visiting my mentor, Maggie DeWoody at her father's farm. Burt DeWoody, Maggie's younger brother was going to take a wagon load of apples to the cider press. The cider press was operated by an itinerant mechanic who traveled throughout the countryside in the "green apple season" with his equipment, consisting of an apple chopper and a squeezer, a few empty barrels and a power plant for the chopper, all loaded into the wagon.

As the press man had set up his business only about a half mile from the DeWoody farm, Maggie suggested to her brother that George (that's me) go along and observe. I climbed into Burt's apple wagon and made myself "comfortable" on that bed of little sour green apples. Burt slapped the reins on the horse's rump and we began that tortuous ride. I said "made myself comfortable" - but imagine, if you can, an empty iron bathtub, now pour a bushel of golf balls into the tub, jump in and sit down. To make the picture more complete, have a Giant jiggle that tub to emulate that bumpy country road over which we were traveling. I couldn't complain of a sore bottom and arrange to take the place of the empty cask which was roped to the seat next to the driver, for I had chosen this "apple-heaven" on my own volition, figuring it would be fun to ride on those little green marbles.

Thank goodness, we did eventually arrive at the pressing scene. Four or five wagons were drawn up around the mill wagon, all loaded with those little green torture balls like our own. I eased myself down from my seat of discomfort and went over to inspect the "mill" – the most prominent part of which was the press standing very high in the rear of the wagon. A box-like structure, made entirely of wood and about eighteen inches square which was topped by a giant wooden screw - reminded me of one of the four wooden posts on the four-poster bed which I used to see in the window of Boyd N. Parks furniture store. On the bed of this wagon, directly in front of this screw-topped monstrosity was the chopper. All I could see of the chopper was a big box with an immense iron wheel sticking out at a crazy angle. The top of the box was open, for, as I soon learned, receiving shovelfuls of apples.

Much more interesting to me was the putt-wheeze, putt-wheeze power plant belted directly via a long, thin, slapping leather belt to that big wheel on the chopper. Burt explained these features to me, but he was called away before I had the opportunity to ask him what made that engine run. It had two big flywheels and looked exactly like the coffee grinder in Higgins' grocery. It was even painted red like the store one, but I couldn't, for the life of me, figure out why they needed a coffee grinder in a cider mill. Besides, this one, unlike Mr. Higgins' grinder kept up that eternal putt-wheeze, putt-wheeze and didn't have to be turned by hand. The whole arrangement was most intriguing and mystifying to me.

One of the other wagons, like our own, filled with those little green apples was pulled up beside the mill wagon and the farmer was scooping up the apples and shoveling them into the chopper box through the open lid. Occasionally the shoveler would stop and direct his attention to the chopped apples which poured out into baskets at the bottom of the chopping box. I couldn't see in the box but I did see that the apples, unwashed, and rotten ones too, came out from the bottom of this box in little pieces like my mother used to cut for apple pie.

Gosh, I thought – dirt, worms, seeds, stems, leaves and twigs, squashed crickets and grasshoppers and many rotten apples were all included in this apple mess. I decided that I didn't want any cider from this farmer's crop. But when it came time for my own apple-riding-cushion to meet the chopper, the same lack of attention to cleanliness was observed. I just didn't care for apple cider anymore.

As the product of the chopper filled each basket it was picked up by hand and emptied into the squeezer. A square wooden grid was dropped into place after three baskets of "mash" and when the press box was full that big screw post was twisted down with an iron rod (also by hand) and the cider poured out of a spout at the bottom and was captured in big, messy iron bound, wooden buckets - the contents of which was, in turn, emptied into a barrel. Didn't believe I liked cider anyhow.

Our own barrel was at last full, still fastened to the wagon seat. Burt clamped a wooden top onto the cask and we drove home. I wondered how Burt knew just how many apples, leaves, twigs and rubble to load into the wagon to produce an exactly, brimful barrel of cider, but then he had done it many times before. I didn't care for cider anymore, anyhow. This time I sat on the floor of the wagon. It was as hard as rock and bumped terrifically, but compared to my ride to the mill it was like heaven.

We arrived back at the farm and after Maggie's father had filled two jugs from our barrel and corked them with corncob stoppers, I watched Burt and his father bail out the cider from the barrel and pour it into an immense iron kettle. A bonfire was made under the kettle and as the cider boiled down, more was added from the barrel. Although the aroma was pleasing, probably because sugar and spices and other things had been added to the pot, I just didn't care much for cider.

I was called in to go to bed before the operation was complete, but I can still see Maggie and her sister Irene taking turns at wielding a big paddle, stirring, ever stirring that boiling caldron of apple juice and other gunk. I found out in the morning that it was on its way to apple butter.

I didn't believe I cared much for apple butter either.

FIDDLESTICKS
(Circa 1902-1903)

And then there was the time when my mother and Mrs. Allen attended a music recital at the Grant's home. Neither was anxious to go, but Mrs. Grant's plea that the neighborhood mothers must take an active interest in the accomplishments of the children finally prevailed.

Most of the performers were pupils of a "Mr. Albert" - whether Albert was his first or his last name, I didn't know. I did hear that he was a struggling bachelor musician, related in some way to the trumpet playing Mr. Brassington, at that time choir director at St. John's church. I also heard that he resided at Mrs. Reid's boarding house on the corner of Fourteenth and Liberty Streets. In any event, Mr. Albert was an itinerant instructor of music - piano, organ, brass and stringed instruments, even vocal lessons were not beyond his many accomplishments. Why he was not referred to as Doctor or Professor Albert was never divulged to me. Just Mr. Albert was the title he apparently preferred.

Many of the student exhibitionists were little girls dressed to perfection, by doting mothers, in frilly laces and ribbons. These child prodigies, to a (man) girl used the piano to distort portions of ambiguous, complex and uninteresting musical pottage. At the conclusion of each rendition, the artist would rise, pivot dexterously on the top of her right heel and curtsy to the dutiful applause of the proud mothers.

The one exception to those who used a piano to hold the audience spellbound was, as I was informed by my mother, a boy named Arlington Peterson who abused a violin as well as the ears of the assembly, with a very mediocre squawking of the first uncertain bars of Beethoven's Moonlight Sonata. Arlington struggled with the piano accompaniment, he struggled with the violin, he struggled with his stiffly starched white collar and finally gave in to superior pressures and relinquished his one-legged pose leaning against the piano. He finally accepted defeat and shook his head in surrender. He was rescued from his dilemma by Mr. Albert, who bowed low to Arlington, thanked him and explained to the guests that Arlington was a recent acquisition of his and he had not had much time to practice that particular piece.

Mrs. Allen was inspired, not by Arlington's performance, but by the thought that her son George, with his winning smile and supple fingers, could well develop into a master of the violin. This, of course, with Mr. Albert to tutor him - plus many, many hours of diligent practice.

In response to the magnificence of this idea, she guided a protesting George on the following day, down Liberty Street to the residence of Mr. Albert who, in response to inquiry, met with mother and son on the front porch of the boarding house, accepted George as a pupil and confirmed his mother's suggestion that George did indeed have long, supple fingers and would probably make an excellent violinist if he could find it in his heart to practice conscientiously.

Our family, led by my father, left the next day for a two weeks vacation in Oak Bluffs, Martha's Vineyard. When we returned home, Mrs. Allen came down to our house. She was exuberant about the progress which George had made with his violin. She addressed my father with this reply to his question as to "Lovely's" struggle with his "catgut" banjo. "Oh, Mr. Stansbury, I have made a schedule of George's hours and he is following it to the letter. Of course it is rather severe, but Mr. Albert has an original saying which he claims is the key to success. He says, 'Practice makes perfect', now isn't that wonderfully original?"

"George arises promptly at six o'clock and practices for an hour before breakfast. After breakfast, he takes a half hour of finger exercises to strengthen the supple fingers of his left hand. Then at nine o'clock, the heavy practice period begins and continues until noon. Then we have lunch and he rests for an hour. At two o'clock, more practice until three thirty. On Tuesdays, Wednesdays and Saturdays he has a session with his instructor. Then a play time until dinner. I still think that adage of 'All work and no play makes Jack a dull boy' should apply to a George as well as a Jack, don't you?

"Then, in the evening, at eight o'clock, George fingers his violin, entertaining the family until it's time for bed. He must have plenty of rest you know."

My father sat in amazement at Mrs. Allen's dissertation on George's complete schedule and his accomplishments. "Well Kate, for how long has 'Lovely' been on this exacting routine?"

"Oh!" says Mrs. Allen, "George starts tomorrow."

THE DESTROYER
(Circa 1902-1903)

And then there was the time when I rummaged around in the attic and found three bed slats lying on the floor. They were back in the cranny between where the roof and the floor met. These slats were just lying there, had been for some time apparently judging from the accumulation of dust on them. I confiscated them and carried them down to the kitchen door and laid them out on the grass outside the kitchen steps. Got two pieces of wood from an old packing box, used these for cross pieces and nailed them all together.

This was the boat. It presumably would float because it was made of wood. Of course the decks would be awash and it couldn't possibly hold Eddie or myself. But there on the solid ground at the back steps it was firm and stable.

In my mind's eye this was a torpedo boat destroyer. But what was a torpedo boat? I hadn't the faintest idea but I assumed, again in my mind's eye, that a torpedo boat was like a canoe with two navy men in it who pelted the enemy ships with those little hickory nut sized, tissue wrapped, independence day torpedoes which could be bought at Rollya's store, packed in a little pasteboard box in a mess of sawdust. They gave off an exaggerated cap pistol report when thrown down on the sidewalk and bits of pea gravel flew back and stung your legs.

Eddie and I had ventured out, on the morning of July the fifth in search of used fireworks. Eddie took the North side of Liberty Street and I took the South side. We walked in the gutters, picking up numerous pieces of spent fireworks, there were roman candles, spent sparklers and devil scooters as well as a few silver colored pasteboard cones which, only yesterday contained the makings of Vesuvius fountains. There was an unpredictable lack of green and red railroad flares which usually supplied us with nice round, pointed, wooden stakes.

A shout from Eddie caused me to drop my armload of burned roman candles and cross the street to examine his find. There, sitting on the curbstone was a big sunburst mine. I immediately knew it was the remains of a sunburst mine because the name SUNBURST was clearly printed on the heavy cardboard cylinder.

Eddie abandoned his other treasures and we hurried home with this piece of pyrotechnic, though used, glory, discussing how we would fasten it to our destroyer to complete the engine room. At Mitchell's we found a burned out pin wheel of exceptional size which we managed to disconnect from the big Oak tree to which it had been nailed. This wheel would make an excellent helm for our powerful ship.

We nailed the mine to the center slat and I ingeniously contrived to mount the wheel at the forward end of the craft so that it could be spun on the attaching nail. A slug of molasses-like harness oil from the gallon can in the barn and a few dead leaves were then dropped into the "boiler." A piece of old tar was added and the contents was thoroughly stirred with a stick and ignited. A smelly, smoky haze was emitted from the "sunburst" boiler now designated the engine room

Imagination can perform miracles, especially when two small boys are involved. I would be the captain. - Hadn't I started the whole project? - Eddie, sitting with the "engine" in front of him would serve as engineer. My position was a sitting one at the front of the vessel, grasping the wheel firmly in both hands. And then we let our fantastic imaginations go rampant.

We would launch the Maggie D. in French Creek and head down stream to the Thirteenth Street bridge at which point I would "port the helm" at the same time calling to the engineer to give us full steam ahead in order to buck the current. Downstream, if we progressed far enough, I knew there was the Allegheny River, but the mysteries of "below the bridge" as well as the uncertainties of just what might be in store for us on the Allegheny, induced me to turn upstream at the bridge. How, just how was that pinwheel loosely attached to the front of our boat going to control direction? More to the point. How was the "smoke pot" under

Eddie's control going to provide power to our destroyer, in the unlikely event that it would float with two men aboard? Neither the lack of rudder nor propeller seemed to matter.

Imagination and the urge for adventure are wonderful panaceas for two fantasy hungry kids. We tentatively decided to launch the Maggie D. on the following morning. Thank goodness Eddie had disclosed our plans to his sister Anna. We had picked up that slat barge and were heading for a launching site on French Creek when Anna screamed at my engineer, "Edward you come right back here this minute or I'll tell Mamma!" That threat took Eddie by surprise and was potent enough to make us turn and give up the proposed adventure.

This shrill admonition from Anna had almost immediately killed any desire the both of us had for further exploration, by water, on the reaches of French Creek. Possibly the Allegheny. THANK YOU Anna.

COWS IS STUPID
(Circa 1902-1903)

And then there was the time when I was up at Bobby Read's house and we were rummaging around in a closet, (Bobby's mother called it a "press") main object being to find missing parts of a long lost Chrokinole[20] game. The big Chrokinole board was present but the little red wooden napkin rings were not.

We weren't having much success in our search and Bobby comes up with, "Say Jimmy have you ever saw my telephone what I got for Christmas?" I admitted I had never seen it and he fumbled around on the top shelf of the ''press" and brought down a fairly large, flat, cardboard box with an elaborate colored picture pasted on the lid.

Bobby explained the picture to me in detail while I impatiently listened. Anyone could see what it was all about. The lithograph showed a little, old lady attired in a brilliant red bathrobe, standing in her home in front of a very ornate wooden door knob which was fastened to the wall of her kitchen. She was undoubtedly speaking into this doorknob. Attached to this knob was a black wire, which, according to the picture, ran through the kitchen wall of the old lady's house and out to the top of a pole in the yard and, as viewed through the kitchen window, the wire extended to the top of another pole an traveled over hill and dale on a series of poles into the very distant horizon.

Anyone with a speck of imagination could see that the old lady was talking to her daughter in the next town by way of the Parsons Autophone. Bobby said that the old lady was asking her husband to bring home a can of beans from the grocery store. I accepted that alternative and suggested that we open the box. Inside were two of those doorknobs, a spool of wire, a packet containing six little, rubber-band sized strips of leather for insulators and six short nails carefully sealed in a wax

---

[20] Chrokinole is a dexterity board game in which players take turns shooting discs across the circular playing surface, trying to have their discs land in the higher-scoring regions of the board, while also attempting to knock away opposing discs.

paper envelope. Also there was a printed sheet of instructions with diagrams of the completed Parsons Auto-phone system.

Those two doorknobs functioned as combination transmitter-receivers - the hookup was like the old tin can and rosin string phones, but not nearly so good. We cut ten feet of the wire from the spool, hooked up the two phones and took turns in shouting to each other across the room. I was enthralled with the clarity of the reception until Bobby pointed out that we could hear just as well across the room without the phones.

"Let's run a line from our barn down to your house," suggested Bobby.

"Wire?" I says.

"I got a whole bunch of it in the barn," says Bob. True. We found a coil of rusty baling wire hanging on a nail and proceeded to string the line from the barn, out to the "first clearing" - to an apple tree and thence down the hill in back of Bigler's and Mom Bridge's - to that tall hickory tree. From there, we cut across the lot to our (Bert's and mine) bedroom window. I drove two big nails in the window sill, spacing them about an inch apart so by taking up the slack in the wire running from the hickory tree, the doorknob could be solidly wedged behind those nails. A minor inconvenience to this arrangement was that the bedroom window had to be left open a few inches. The window sash would crush the knob if it was suddenly pushed down. So What?

Brother Bert saw the nails with the "instrument" in place. He immediately advised me that he was going to shut the window at night. My appeals to him for fair play were ignored. I thought of nailing the window open when Bert wasn't present, but he just stayed close and he was bigger than me. Well that evening I slipped the receiver out of it's two nail socket an dropped it out of the window.

Next morning I lowered a "recovery" string from the window and went out side to tie it to the knob. No knob! I solved by deduction, what had happened. Regardless of appearances, I must have been a smart cookie. Moppy Smith had driven his two cows up to pasture early in the morning. The cows, having little or no scientific training, had stumbled across the downed phone wire and Moppy, observing the doorknob hastening across the field on the ground, and also being somewhat of a laggard in his modern science studies, had removed the wire and pocketed the knob.

I was mad at Moppy. I was mad at the cows. I was mad at Bert, but Bobby wasn't mad at me. His comment, on learning of the disaster was, "Oh Jimmy it don't matter none to me, the darn phones wouldn't work anyway." Then he added, "But didn't we have fun stringin' the line?"

THE COMIC
(Circa 1902-1903)

And then there was the time when Bert and I had apparently worried our mother to the point of distraction. She, in desperation, had recalled seeing an ad in the Franklin Evening News which promoted a play. (I say play because that is what the ad called it) Jumble would probably been a more appropriate choice of wording. This, so called, play was to be put on by a road company which made a two performance stop in our entertainment hungry little town. A matinee, and, if the take was not too disappointing, an evening show of the same feature.

My mother gave Bert forty cents, the price of two admissions to the matinee and sent us off to the show for what we, mother included, promised to be an afternoon of pleasure. At Bert's behest we walked down Buffalo Street to Thirteenth, turned left and were in the lobby of that wonderful center of culture and amusement The Franklin Opera House. I was not particularly impressed with the dignity of the auditorium next door to the Franklin Fire Department, nor was I awed by the splendor of the stage and tasseled curtain, although this was my first introduction to the inside of a real theatre. What did impress me was the magnificent accoutrement[21] of the man who took up the tickets. He was red faced, red headed and he wore a uniform of scarlet with the word BAND embroidered in gold on each lapel. My goodness, he was the epitome of all that I could imagine was the glamour of show business.

We took seats near the center in the fifth row. I wanted to go down to the front row, which was practically vacant, but Bert whispered to me that the projection was not good in the front row. I didn't know what projection was, but hoped that Bert did. Hadn't he used the word?

The expectant thrill of witnessing my first real curtain raising was something I'll never forget. The orchestra, four or five men, dressed in those vivid scarlet uniforms played a few bars of "Rag Time Gal" and

---

[21] Additional items of dress or equipment, or other items carried or worn by a person or used for a particular activity:

92

the curtain went up. A man and a woman conversed in rather loud voices and rushed erratically around the stage. I tried to gather what they were talking about but after a few moments of frustration, poking my brother on the arm and in a hushed tone inquiring of him, "What'd he say, what'd he say?" I gave up and attempted to count the plaster gargoyle faces on the large picture frame which bordered the stage curtain. I referred to it, in a whisper, to Bert as "that picture frame." He whispered back to me that it was not a frame but, as I understood him, a procinnamon arch.[22] I studied this arch again, trying to determine why it was called cinnamon. The little brown sparkles on the gold frame looked something like the cinnamon which I sprinkled on my rice with sugar at lunch time. I was satisfied.

The curtain was lowered again after, Bert's interpretation, "The end of the first act." Then the red faced, red haired man who had collected our tickets at the door, came down the aisle and took his place in the band. It was like seeing an old friend, for I was so bored with the "play" up to this point. The resplendent one's duties as ticket taker were over for the matinee, and now he was a slide trombonist in the orchestra. Was there no limit to the accomplishments of this man? I decided at that moment that this was what I wanted to be when I grew up - a combination ticket taker and trombonist in a theatrical company - and getting to wear a brilliant red uniform too. Oh the vagaries of youth!

The drop was again lifted and what (to me) was the climax of the whole performance took place. The comic (Bert called him that) appeared wearing a clown suit. He strutted to the front of the stage and mumbled something about being late for an appointment, then he, with a great flourish, reached back and produced an alarm clock from his hip pocket, exclaiming in a loud voice that ''I'm not late, I 'm ahead of time.''

This, I say was the funniest and most understandable move that had been made or attempted on the stage. I spent the rest of the afternoon going over this bit of hilarity in my mind and paid no more attention to

---

[22] Referring to the proscenium arch: an arch framing the opening between the stage and the auditorium in some theaters.

the rest of the performance. I reviewed this joke over and over in my think box. See, the man thought he was late but pulled the clock (time) from out of his back pocket and thereby proved that he was in front (ahead) of time. I had figured this clever piece of monolog out all by myself. Gee I was smart! I had figured the whole move alone and was pleased with my own discernment.

I considered using this gag in one of our home exhibitions with Mary, Katy and Bobby Read as an audience. But first, I would try it out on my mother to get her reactions to my ingenuity.

After arriving home and answering the routine questions, directed at Bert and me by my mother, I contemplated the loud mouthed alarm clock which hung on a nail over the kitchen sink. It was too big and besides I didn't have a hip pocket. I hurried up to my room, rooted through the bureau drawer and found one of my once most precious possessions, a one dollar Ingersoll watch. Once most precious, is literally true, For my father had bought it for me on one of his numerous trips to New York. I had entrusted to him my brand new silver dollar Christmas present. He handed me the watch and then said, "And here's your change Donkey," tossing a copper cent to me. He had happened into Macy's during a sale and Ingersoll watches were priced at ninety nine cents. After two days of winding, setting and displaying the watch I perfunctorily dropped it into the toilet bowl from which it was promptly recovered by my mother, but not promptly enough to keep it from stopping and allowing rust to take charge.

Without a hip pocket from which to pull the watch, I held it at arms length behind me in order to test the comic's joke on my mother. She was not particularly impressed with the performance even when I explained that I thought that I was behind, but now had proved that I was ahead of time. My own active mind was apparently just too clever for my own mother's understanding. But I discarded both the idea and the watch.

Oh well, you can't win them all. I assumed that the joke wasn't quite as good as I had at first thought.

JUST A SIMPLE SNITCH?
(Circa 1902-1903)

And then there was the time when, about the first week in February, when Shorty Evans asked Bert to go on a valentine snitch with him. I had no idea what that meant and neither did Bert at the time. Of course "grab" or "hook" was the common term for purloin - snitch had not yet invaded the Franklin territory but was well known in Cincinnati, as we discovered a few years later. How Shorty was so well informed I'll never know.

Shorty and his innocent partner in crime went to town and sought refuge near the back of a store where they sold notions, maybe Rollya's, maybe Joe Riesenman's drug store maybe the great Woodburn department store. I just don't know which store it was so I won't confuse the issue by assuming that I do. You see I hadn't been invited to go along.

The so called comic valentines in those days consisted of a single sheet of eight by eleven, cheap, off-white paper on which was imprinted a somewhat ghastly witch, an animal or perhaps a flop-eared and distressingly ugly individual. The sheet also sported a poem, unpleasant, often vicious and most uncomplimentary description of the intended victim, who was to be the recipient. The whole unsavory item was not, in most stores, displayed for sale at a prominent place where the real valentines held counter space, lacy, frilly confections professing love for the person lucky enough to receive one. These "comics," disreputable, nasty versions of valentines usually had a position of their own in the back reaches of the store, where only persons with such uncouth tastes sought them out.

It was to this hole of depravity that Shorty led Bert, thumbed through stacks of these "comics," telling Bert that he was looking for a picture of a particularly obnoxious "witch." He advised Bert that he wanted this special "pitcher" complete with verse to slip under the door of "Old Lady Wernicke" because she had "hoity-toitied" his brother

96

Ralph out of the yard simply because Ralph was innocently inspecting the Wernicke grape arbor. Gosh but that was last year! How long could LeRoy bear a grudge?

As Shorty "thumbed" he stuffed a great many fistfuls of the valentines into his shirt front and urged brother Bert to do likewise. "Come on, don't be ascared, that's wot they want you to do."

Bert declined the invitation and was not at all tempted to favor Shorty's tactics, especially after noting a card on the counter, which Shorty had tried to conceal. The card said simply: "COMICS 2 for 1¢." Bert had not been brought up that way, but continued badgering by Shorty finally induced him to sneak the top sheet from the nearest bundle, crumple it hastily and shove it into his pants pocket, more to let his companion see that he was willing to accept a dare than because he approved of the routine. Best take Shorty's account of the incident which was told to me that evening, "Yeh, I finely got him to snitch one, you'da thought he'd robbed the Exchange Bank - his face got so red it lit up the whole store so's I thought mebbe the place was afire!"

And then my brother Bert came home that afternoon with a rather chagrined look on his face. He pulled a crumpled and wadded "comic" from his pocket, tore it into bits and admitted to me that Shorty had made him do it. All in all, he and I both concluded that the afternoon's "snitch" episode had been a complete bust.

THAT LANTERN
(Circa 1902-1903)

And then there was the time when Eddie Riesenman was out in our side yard with his little toy tin lantern. It was just growing dark and Eddie was gyrating his lighted lantern, and himself, emulating a railroad brakeman giving signals to the engineer. I wondered, at the time, when Eddie had ever had the opportunity to watch a railroad man swing his lantern. He was, at all times, confined to our immediate neighborhood, i.e. his own home and yard and that of his next door neighbor, me.

Poor Eddie was put to bed promptly at nine every evening, as was I. But he never enjoyed the opportunity of wandering from the overseeing eye of his mother or Anna, an older sister. How then could he possibly pick up this ability to translate railroader's signals, especially as performed with a lantern at night? He couldn't, as I soon learned.

When I first approached him that evening in the driveway between our two houses, he was whirling the lantern in merry-go-round circles over his head and he accompanied these gyrations with lively foot work, twirling himself in dizzying circles to keep pace with the overhead swinging of the light. I inquired of him (trying to be funny) if he was doing this to attract lightning bugs. "Haw," says Eddie, "this is a railroad signal. It means all aboard."

Now, those little kerosene lanterns came in three parts, any or all of which could be purchased from Rollya's store at five cents apiece. Or you could obtain the assembled equipment for a total outlay of fifteen cents. The three parts of the lantern were - (1) the base, or tank with wick and complex mechanism for adjusting the same. (2) The glass globe through which the flame was seen. This globe, or chimney, had threads at both ends, not unlike the threads on a Mason jar. This chimney came in either clear or ruby red glass. And (3) the hat or top, which screwed onto the uppermost part of the chimney. This had had a wire bail attached. The bail was for the purpose of carrying the lantern, or, in

98

Eddie's case, to swing it. I often wondered why the tank third of this consolidation, with the complexities of its wick and adjuster didn't have a higher price put on it than either the glass or the hat. But we won't worry about that now.

The chimney of Eddie's lantern I noticed, was blackened and sooty inside. Eddie probably had the wick "turner upper" far too high. So I approached him and attempted to lower the flame. The "turner upper" was jammed and I recommended that we take the top off, blow out the flame and determine what was the trouble. We went into the kitchen of my house - Eddie was allowed that much leeway - put the lantern in the sink, unscrewed the top, blew out the flame, and remarking that we'd better wash the chimney while we had the thing apart, to which, (note) Eddie half-heartedly agreed. I pushed the hatless lantern under the faucet and turned on the water.

Then, in the dimly lighted kitchen, as the evening shadows fell, all hell broke loose. Need I tell you more? There was the hiss of steam, one resoundingly sharp report as though a gun had been fired at point blank range where the lantern stood in the sink. This was followed by the tinkling of broken glass mingled with Eddie's high pitched screams of dismay. This brought my mother, post haste, to the scene of the calamity. I put on an act, assured mother that everything was alright and I got Eddie to quit his wailing.

But I was petrified, even though I attempted to put up a calm appearance to mother, so now I turned to Eddie who was now standing behind me and still quietly whimpering, "Oh don't worry Eddie, everything is got 'ta be dandy. Wait 'till I get some light." Still in a state of shock, I climbed up on the drain board of the sink, from which point I could reach the valve of the Welsback[23] light fixture. I turned it up and put more brilliance on the broken fragments of that hapless chimney in the sink. "Don't worry Eddie," I repeated, "I'll buy you a new chimney

---

[23] Welsbach was a brand of gas lighting fixtures.

tomorrow." And then, letting my sense of the beneficent get the better of good judgement, I added, "In fact I'll buy you a red one too."

Need I add that I still haven't replaced, to this day, that smashed chimney, much less a red one too?

Although Eddie frequently reminded me of my promise, I considered that I was only partially to blame. If Eddie hadn't been playing in my side yard, if he hadn't twirled the lantern over his head so fast, if he had adjusted the flame properly, so as not to blacken the chimney, and if he hadn't been so agreeable and vociferous in accepting my suggestion that we adjust the wick and wash the chimney - well he would still have his dirty tin lantern anyway.

ME, A WITNESS?
(Circa 1902-1903)

And then there was the time when the sound coming from outside our house was something like a wooden snow shovel being used haltingly to clear a path to the kitchen door, "schizz" pause, "schizz" pause, "schizz." Being a boy of unusual brightness and perception, I instantly realized that the month was either July or August and therefore it could not possibly be someone shoveling snow.

So I went to the back door. There was Eddie Riesenman standing in the alcove at the side of his house busily picking up handful after handful of sand from a "happenstance" sand pile and hurling it at the screened window of his pantry. He was diligent and apparently devoted to his work, scraping up a handful of sand, then stepping back from the house to get a better aim, and throwing the sand with unerring accuracy against that screened window, "schizz" pause, "schizz" pause. "Schizz" was the noise made by the sand as it came into violent contact with the screen.

I went to the kitchen door and asked Eddie why he was doing this. He glared at me and muttered something about his sister Anna and his mother having gone to visit his Uncle Ed. "and they wouldn't take me, they even took Mildurd," he whimpered. I knew that Eddie must be in dire straits for he referred to his sister as "Mildurd," customarily he called her "Liz." Eddie was, perhaps, being punished for some indiscretion which he had committed or for some task which he had failed to perform that morning. At any rate, I deduced that he was angry at the whole world. Seeing that it would be impossible for me, just a next-door neighbor and sometime playmate to soothe his feelings, I ended the conversation with a word of caution for his wellbeing.

"You better be sure that window is closed," I ventured, "or else your pantry will be full of sand."

"Sopen," muttered Eddie and continued with his task, "schizz" pause, "schizz" pause, "schizz."

101

One thing was apparent, whatever sand accumulated in the pantry would a be small grained and thoroughly sifted. I retired to the kitchen, sponsoring the happy thought that I had done everything possible to alleviate the severity of Eddie's definitely forthcoming punishment.

He continued with his work of grabbing up handfuls of sand, pebbles and dirt and propelling them against that defenseless screen window. (I watched his endeavors from our own pantry window.) He worked diligently at this task and did not stop until that little triangular pile of leftover construction sand was reduced to its pebble content.

Then, Eddie's mother and sisters, Anna and Mildred, arrived home from their visit. Mrs. Riesenman probably went immediately to the second floor. Mildred, I saw crawling under the back porch in search of her brother, who had taken refuge there at the first indication of his returning family. Mildred, of course, knew all of her brother's hideouts and must have gone to the kitchen by way of the pantry, for I heard her scream to her mother, "Mama come here and look at this pantry, everything is full of sand!"

Mother rushed down to the pantry and immediately appeared at that fateful window. "Edward," she shrieked, "Edward did you do this? There is dirt on the floor, dirt on the shelves and dirt in my rice pudding, why there is even dirt in the sugar bowl! Edward come here this instant!"

Eddie crept slowly from under the kitchen porch. Mildred, on hands and knees peered out at the great outdoors, not knowing whether to abandon the safety of her present retreat. Although she was blameless in this particular instance, she didn't like to be in range when Mother lost her temper. "What you want?" asks Eddie, putting on the guise of total innocence. He feigned complete ignorance of the whole affair. "Were could all that sand have come from?"

Here was my opportunity to become the hero of this, fast-developing, melodrama. To be the star witness, the only one who could give a full account of the disaster. I stepped to our kitchen door and called out in clear, vibrant tones, "Eddie did it Mrs. Reisenman, I saw

102

him do it.'' And then grasping the full importance of my position and well being in that enviable spot of front center stage, I added, "I told him not to do it, but he just kept on doing it."

This statement of mine was based on the truth even though it was a bit stretched. I had suggested to Eddie that the window should be closed, I had not exactly told him to stop, but in my position as the leading witness and possibly head prosecutor it wasn't necessary to be absolutely truthful in every detail. Besides, I hadn't promised to tell the whole truth and nothing but.

The sudden elevation to star witness, I'm afraid, gave me a false sense of power and superiority. As I heard poor Eddie's screams from an upstairs bedroom, each scream punctuated by the whack of a well-placed hair brush, I retired to the parlor with a feeling of a martyr who had given his everything to promote worldly good. - Gosh! Wasn't I a little stinker?

THE PARADE
(Circa 1902-1903)

And then there was the time when I was chosen by LeRoy (Shorty) Evans to act the part of the wild man of Borneo in our neighborhood production (parade only) of that vicious personality. John Robinson's circus had recently visited our fair city. The vivid posters had proclaimed that their ten big shows were world shattering, stupendous, wonders that had never before been viewed by mankind. These all could be seen within the confines of their "all inclusive" three ring tent.

However, the wild man of Borneo did not appear in the "all inclusive" big tent. He was a side show attraction and Shorty had ingratiated himself in the eyes and thoughts of the wild man's barker[24] by chasing a few pestering little kids from the premises. Consequently he, Shorty, was invited to view the side show, free of any monetary consideration. And so Shorty was the instigator, as well as the overall authority on the choice of characters and raiment of the wild man and his entourage, for he, and only he, had seen the original himself.

First, my animated facial features were smeared with the sooty end of a partially burned cork. Then I was garmented in an old rubber mackintosh which had been found hanging from a nail in the Read's barn. Peough, it was stinky and smelled horsey and somewhat like manure, although there hadn't been a horse in that barn in all of my memory. Gosh I was hot. A trunk strap was borrowed from our attic and attached to my middle, much too tightly for comfort. An old piece of rope was knotted to the strap at my waist line. Thus the free end of the trunk strap and the loose part of the rope made it possible for brother Bert and Shorty to lead me, the wild man, at a safe distance, Shorty on the end of the strap and Bert holding the rope. This procedure made it possible for them to contain the wild man between them. If I lunged for

---

[24] A person who stands in front of a theater, sideshow, etc., and calls out to passersby to attract customers.

104

Shorty, Bert could restrain me by tightening up on the rope, or if I got too close to Bert, Shorty could hold me from doing bodily harm to Bert by jerking on the strap.

Shorty surveyed the results of his artistry with a quizzical eye, decided that I would look more ferocious it I flaunted a knife in one hand. An old, rusty butcher knife was procured from the pantry treasure drawer and given to me. A second inspection by Shorty brought out the fact that I didn't quite meet the requirements of the wild man, so a hastily daubed sign was fastened to a broom and Bobby Read was delegated to carry this sign and precede me on the march. The sign certified that, I indeed was the real Wild Man of Borneo. Ralph, Shorty's little brother, was given an old dish pan an a stick to beat it with for the purpose of summoning the potential spectators.

Then we started out, down Elk Street, Ralph, beating vigorously on the pan, then came the sign bearer followed by the main attraction, the wild man himself guided by his two fearless keepers, both of whom were pulling in opposite directions on the restraining shackles. I wonder now whether the reason they kept their distance from the wild man was to hold him at bay or rather to keep as far away from that odorous rubber coat which encased him. Oh Golly was I hot!

I surmised that my image was dashing. The sweat rolled down my face smearing my homemade mascara into rivulets and dark brown streaks. Gosh I was hot. I must have presented a picture of a burly, vigorous, healthy and well muscled athlete of African descent to all who saw me. A viciously brutal and robust man, held captive, but constantly scheming to escape. At least that is the realistic conclusion which I reached concerning myself - so enraptured had I become with the part I was playing in this childhood parade.

Our first stop was at a little cottage surrounded by a once-white picket fence. The lady of the house was sitting in her front yard entertaining two young children. She had a pitcher of milk and a plate of graham crackers on an improvised table at her side.

The parade halted to satisfy the youngsters' curiosity. The woman approached us from the far side of the picket fence and after surveying me, she remarked that I looked undernourished and sick, offered me a glass of milk and a couple of graham crackers. I, following instructions, brandished my butcher knife at her and declared that I was not hungry - "But thank you just the same."

Gosh it was hot, and stinky too. Whether I took my cue from the lady or not I fail to remember, but suddenly I did feel desperately ill. I pleaded with my captors to let me rest. Bert realized that I was not feeling too good and immediately stopped dragging me from side to side with the rope. Shorty, on the other hand, kept jerking on his end of my restraining strap. He did not wish to give up on his dream of a self-made and, up till now, successful parade. Gosh it was hot in that rubber coat. The trunk strap was too tight and that continuous, erratic pulling from side to side made me nauseous.

With Bert's help, I finally convinced Shorty that I must be released. The belt was removed, I shed the filthy rubber coat and dropped it and my dastardly machete at the sidewalk's edge, sat down with my back propped against that weathered picket fence, and proceeded to be sick.

Thus ended that memorable parade. Shorty walked away, thoroughly disgusted. He mumbled something to the effect that this was the last time he would lend his time and talent to making a bunch of amateurs act like professionals. I was sick and didn't fully realize whether he was complementing us or censuring us. Besides, I wasn't familiar with either the term professional nor amateur.

Bert helped me home. Golly it was still hot. Ralph could not believe that the festivities were concluded, beat on his pan and preceded Bert and me home.

RADISHES FOR TILLIE
(Circa 1902-1903)

And then there was the time when mother handed Bert a packet of radish seeds and suggested that we boys, Bert and I, plant them in the level ground below the barn. We eagerly accepted the seeds and the idea.

But first the garden had to be prepared. We had only one very rusty pick and a short handled scoop - used to clean out the cow's stall. I wasn't much good at gardening anyway. So Bert wielded the pick and I lazily dragged the clods down with the scoop. Eddie Riesenman joined us. He wasn't any more ambitious than I was, but he did have a rake with which Bert was able to smooth out this little garden plot while Eddie and I watched.

The seeds were planted. In a couple of weeks, inspection revealed that those radishes were really sprouting. So Bert, in his usual "big-business-way" (he must have inherited it from the Hatcher-side of the family)[25] called for a meeting of the minds, himself, Eddie, (Bert had used Eddie's rake) and me.

With all of these radishes coming on, we must arrange to sell some. He assigned to Eddie the territory on Liberty Street from Fifteenth to Sixteenth including our side of Sixteenth Street. Eddie protested that we wouldn't have enough radishes to fill all of the orders in that vast territory. He finally prevailed on Bert to cut out all except the Barnes, the Wernickes and his own home. I was to call on the Bridges, Gleason's (that was before the Biglers moved in) and the Berlin's. No need to contact the Allen's for Herb Allen was a "home student" for horticulture and probably supplied his own family with plenty of radishes. Bert would sell to the lady of the house at the Stansbury's. The price was set at a nickel a bunch. No bunch size was designated.

So we set out, Eddie and I in opposite directions on Sixteenth Street. Eddie was back before I really got started, I was a dilly-dallier.

---

[25] Referring to Alice Lincoln Hatcher, his mother.

He reported that no one was at home at the Barnes' and he was afraid to visit Wernicke's because the house was set so far back from the street, and as far as his own home was concerned, he believed that he would give his share of the radishes to his mother.

I prevailed upon Eddie to accompany me on my rounds of soliciting. We climbed the many stone steps to "Mom" Bridge's house, went to the back door and I hesitantly knocked. "Mrs. Bridge, please we are taking orders for radishes." I spoke as one in authority, trying to impress Eddie I suppose. "You wouldn't want any would you?"

"Well yes. I'll have some George," she says. "How much are they?"

"They're a nickel a bunch but we can't deliver them for a day or two."

"You wait right here George and I'll get the money!" In spite of my protests, she went inside, returned and forced me to accept a nickel. Eddie, who had been cringing in the background while I was making the sales pitch now came out from behind the corner of the house, asked to see the "take" and became ecstatic when I showed him the nickel. We then went back home, feeling that our accomplishment merited the rest of the day off.

I presume that we had planted those radishes a bit late in the growing season for a bunker crop. No matter how often Bert and I inspected the garden, (four or five times a day) and although the foliage advanced to a luxuriant green, the roots remained miniature for days. They finally reached the stage of a kitchen match head.

And then to add to my predicament, we (big brother Peedubya[26], Bert and I) were about to accompany our father and mother on a two weeks vacation to Aunt Lou's River Styx summer home at Lake Hopatcong.[27] That nickel which I had accepted from Mrs. Bridge weighed heavily on my conscience. I hoped against hope that she would forget it completely, almost came to the unthinkable conclusion that I

---

[26] Referring to his brother P.W.

[27] Lake Hopatcong is the largest freshwater body in New Jersey

should return the money with proper apologies for being unable to make delivery of the groceries. This solution was, of course, now impossible, for I had spent the nickel for a package of Beeman's pepsin gum and had generously given to Bert and Eddie one stick each.

Time was growing short and I must act. So I approached the radish bed hopefully, pulled about a dozen of those little red match heads with the long tails. Was careful to preserve the green foliage, for that would make the completed bunch appear to be larger than it really was. I say that I pulled about a dozen, due to our frequent testings for maturity, that's all there were to be found. Took them into the kitchen, gave them a quick rinse and tied them into one nosegay[28] sized cluster.

Then with trembling knees, I again climbed those endless stone steps to Mom Bridge's house. I did this all alone. All my urging of brother Bert, and Eddie to go with me was to no avail. Neither of them would accompany me, they both had important business elsewhere.

Timidly I knocked at the back door, handed Mrs. Bridge the bouquet with a, "Here's your radishes," and fled wildly, not back down that precarious flight of stone steps, but through her back yard, underneath the crabapple tree, over the fence and home.

Gardening, I concluded, was for the birds.

---

[28] A small bunch of flowers, typically one that is sweet-scented.

THAT THERE BEAUTIFUL CARBON ELECTRODE[29]
(Circa 1902-1903)

And then there was the time when I was standing on our front lawn watching the streetlight man fixing that big hanging arc lamp at the end of Liberty Street. He unlocked the reel on the pole in front of McCalmont's house with a little round key. Put his iron crank on one end of the reel, turned it and lowered that lamp to within a few feet of the ground. The lamp, with it's umbrella-like black iron roof looked enormous when it was lowered.

Don Allen, who knew most everything, had told me that the man was Tom Carter and that he was a member of the fire department and if a fire alarm was turned in while he was working on one of those street lamps, Tom would drop everything and run to the fire. Golly! How I wished that scary fire department bell would ring right now and I could see Tom fly.

He wiped out the glass globe of the lamp, took the two little pieces of used carbon rod out and dropped them in the street. Then he reached down to his big leather sack and pulled out of it, two long, black colored sticks of new carbon and affixed them in place, returned to the reel and cranked the lamb back up into position.

As soon as he left, I rushed out into the street and retrieved those two little pieces of "black chalk." Stopping at the corner I drew a picture of a locomotive on one of the big square stone slabs which made up the sidewalk. What a mess I always made of the cowcatcher![30] It never seemed to have any depth and never looked much like a cowcatcher anyhow. This was a great many years before my big brother P.W. first began to glamorize his school books with little illustrations of railroad trains travelling at break-neck speed across the countryside and across the tops of the book pages. If these drawings with the elliptical wheels,

---

[29] This piece was most likely written in the mid 1970's.

[30] A metal frame at the front of a locomotive for pushing aside cattle or other obstacles on the line.

denoting speed, had been available at that time I would not have needed assistance from anyone in drawing a cowcatcher. But just then another master artist, Harold Osmer, followed by his little brother Gilbert came across the street from "Grandma's" house on their way home. Both Harold and Gilbert were leading their little iron-tired velocipedes[31] by the handlebars. I just couldn't understand why they didn't ride them on the sidewalk between "Grandma's" house and home. On one occasion, I questioned Harold about this, even offered to ride his for him down to the steps in front of Barnes' house. He replied that he didn't know why, just he would rather walk. He did not accept my offer to ride it for him and I would have liked to ride that velocipede more than anything.

Harold, on this journey, stopped to view my picture of a locomotive and without a word he accepted my proffered "chalk" and drew, with a few simple strokes, a cowcatcher which looked amazingly like a cowcatcher. I asked him to do it again and he slapped another cowcatcher on that stone slab with uncanny adroitness and precision. Then, followed by Gilbert, he led his velocipede towards home.

I studied Harold's drawing in the minutest detail and finally was able to almost duplicate it.

That business of having to use pieces of "chalk" when that Mr. Carter had a whole big leather pouch full of those "new sticks" sorta got me. I contemplated, time and time again, getting up nerve enough to approach him and humbly ask for a new stick of "chalk" but I always backed down when the time arrived. I consulted Don Allen. He suggested that if I asked Tom in a nice way, he would be glad to give me one of those long electrodes. I pondered this suggestion. You know I'd like to have a new stick of "chalk" almost as badly as I wanted to ride Harold Osmer's velocipede. Don suggested that if I was too chicken to ask Tom for a new stick that I could swipe one out of that big leather pouch when Tom wasn't looking. I vetoed this idea. Considered it might be dishonest.

---

[31] A human-powered land vehicle with one or more wheels. The most common type of velocipede today is the bicycle.

111

But I was determined to ask. Finally the day of the challenge arrived. It was Thursday, the day Mr. Carter came to change the carbon sticks in that street lamp. I waited on the terrace of our front yard from eight in the morning until almost noon, thinking of when the critical moment came how I would conduct the request exercise. Calling him "Tom" would be impertinent. Calling him Mr. Carter would sound less familiar, but I had never spoken to the man before. So I guessed I'd just call him "Mister." "Mister" finally arrived, cranked down the lamp, wiped out the globe, dropped the two short, used pieces of "chalk" in the street, selected two new pieces from the pouch, adjusted them and returned to the wind-up reel. I would have to act fast, so throwing caution to the winds, I sauntered across to the corner and bracing myself for the ordeal, I mumbled, "Please Mister, could I have a piece of new chalk?"

Without a word he reached down and pulled beautiful, fresh carbon from that pouch and handed it to me. I managed a very timid "Thank you," and sped back to the home terrace. Golly, I was happy! Tried the new "chalk" out on the cream colored siding of our house. It squeaked and didn't write nearly as well as the used pieces and it was too long to handle easily. Anyway, I now owned them, and that was gratifying.

The next day Don Allen, with a complete reversal of form, told me about a man who had "borrowed" a piece of wire from the electric light plant and was now spending a week in jail, "Better dot let doughbody see you with that carbod stick," cautioned Don. Even though it had been given to me, I was scared. Calling to mind that the "Boston Iron Works" where we kids occasionally sold junk wouldn't accept railroad iron, because even so insignificant an item as a bent spike, which sometimes got into our treasure box, would be quickly spotted by the Boston man and removed from the salvage before the weigh-in.

"That spike," he would say, "is railroad propitty, I don't by no railroad propitty."

Well now! Maybe the fresh new long carbon sticks, which I considered my own, which had been given to me by an employee of the light company, maybe those sticks still belonged to the company. Maybe I would be seen with them someday and brought to account. Maybe Tom had no more right to give them to me than I had the right to accept them, even though Tom was a member in good standing of the Franklin Fire Department. - I was worried.

Questions and doubts filled my nimble brain. Answers were few as well as precarious. I might attempt to slip the carbon rods back into Tom's leather pouch - too hazardous - and if he saw me he would consider that I was just an ungrateful little snob, might even tell me so. I might destroy their long, sleek look by breaking them into small pieces with a rock. The very thought of spoiling the pristine elegance made my inborn appreciation for manufactured beauty rebel. I just could not smash them.

S-o-o, I crawled under the front porch with them, into that dark, spidery retreat, where, on rare occasions, I was tempted to hide when the world was not treating me as affably as I figured it should. Carefully, I tucked them away on a level 2x4 scantling against the side wall of that desolate place.

I squeezed out from under the porch again into the bright summer sunlight and tried to forget all about it. I wonder if the beautiful, carbon electrodes are still there? Well why not? Yes even after seventy two or seventy three years I bet those electrodes are still as beautiful as ever and still resting comfortably in their under-the-porch hideout. Wouldn't I like to find out?

THOSE COLORED SILKS
(Circa 1902-1903)

And then there was the time when our mother and father had taken Bert and me to an evening performance of Harry Kellar, the magician. Imagine Kellar had a one night stand in the opera house in our little town - can't be sure but engagements were rather sparse in those days, especially for magicians.

This was long before Howard Thurston had teamed up with him. Kellar started his act with "The Obedient Ball" which rolled up and down a spiral metal track, starting and stopping at his command. Following this, there were numerous card tricks and the magic rose bush. Then Harry went into, what I considered his prettiest and most elusive piece of prestidigitation. He waved a white silk handkerchief slowly, at arms length and suddenly a red handkerchief joined the white one. Continued waving brought out a blue one and a yellow one, from nowhere! It was amazing and thoroughly impossible!

Cabinet appearances, disappearances, levitation and the sealed trunk which was suspended from the balcony rail all during the performance and was finally slid down to the stage on a rope trolley and was opened, to reveal an almost naked woman who bowed and cavorted to the delight of the audience and gave no indication of having been doubled up in that sealed trunk all during the performance. These were all mystifying and beautifully executed. But the sight of those colored handkerchiefs appearing from nowhere was a magnificent illusion, and in my judgment, was the real mystery and most astounding feature of the entire show.

The next day, I was discussing the thrill and glamor of his mysticism with Clarence Coffin, who had also gone on the previous night to see Harry Kellar's performance. We were joined by a mutual friend William Lewis (not related to the Colonel, his wife or naturally their daughter, Pussy.) William was a quiet reserved boy, he was always addressed as William, never Bill or Willy. Something about his attitude and quiet demeanor would not permit these more friendly monikers.[32] So all his boyhood friends, even though he was well liked, called him William.

On this occasion, William scoffed at Kellar's magic and remarked that anyone could do as much if they had sold their soul to the devil, as Kellar had undoubtedly done. This story (although I recognized it as probably untrue) prompted me to inquire of William just how he knew that Kellar had made such a deal with the devil. "Cause my father told me so," says William, and left Clarence and me to continue our discussion.

That night in reviewing the day's happenings, I came to the conclusion that if William's father was really sincere in his statement, that I too, would be glad to sell my soul to the devil if he would show me how to make those various colored handkerchiefs appear from nowhere. How to get in touch with the devil was my immediate problem.

The next day, I met William alone at noon and asked him pointedly, how to go about getting an audience with the devil. William replied that he personally didn't know but he would ask his father about it. Then on Thursday morning, I again found William alone (he was not a mingler). He told me that his father was not absolutely sure of all of the details, but he did know that, if a person really wanted to talk to the devil, he would have to fast for twelve days and he would be obliged to drink a big glassful of vinegar on each of the twelve days he was fasting. I thanked William for the information and went home to mull it over. The fasting, I figured would not be much of a handicap. But where was I going to get all of that vinegar?

Finally I decided that this would be impossible without revealing the secret to my mother and so I abandoned the idea completely. Didn't really believe that Kellar was instructed by the devil anyhow. Although his advertising posters showed a very red Lucifer whispering secrets

---

[32] Monikers are names.

into Harry's attentive ear. And I did, so much, want to be able to perform that one beautiful trick with the white handkerchief.

Many years later, I discovered how this particular piece of magic was accomplished. I found, by reading between the lines of a Johnson and Co. magic catalogue which referred to handkerchiefs as "silks" that the devil had nothing whatsoever to do with it. Needless to say, I was happy about the whole thing.

THE VOICE OF AUTHORITY
(Circa 1902-1903)

And then there was the time when Bert and I dragged our little white wooden sleds out to the sidewalk in front of our house. My sled, the "Snow Bird," was a smaller edition of brother Bert's "Snow King," both sleds were bright, white, shining and new. The only difference was in size and the name inscribed on the enameled surface - and in the little wooden banister type hand grips at the side, above the runners. Mine had only a single, short rail, while Bert's was twice as long. Oh those two companion sleds were beautiful.

Bert took off down the icy Liberty Street sidewalk, McCalmont's side, while I (having a more conservative nature) dragged the Snow Bird up the Sixteenth Street sidewalk to "Mom" Bridges front gate and slid back down the icy walk "belly buster" until we, Snow Bird and I, came to a stop at our own front steps. Determined to elaborate on the experience, I decided to go further up the hill, maybe to Victor Bigler's house. I turned around at the Bigler's front steps and surveyed the route back. Gollies - that hill was steep! And the sidewalk was slippery and narrow. I contemplated pulling the sled to the middle of snow covered Sixteenth Street and starting from there, but the snow was too deep for Snow Bird's runners. Bert, in the mean time, had probably zipped down Liberty to Fourteenth or thereabouts.

Bobby and Katy Read were playing "Fox and Goose"[33] on a necessarily small, pie-shaped path trampled in the snow of their front yard. Katy called to me, "Jimmy come on up and play, you can be the fox if you'll come." I explained to her that I was trying out my new Christmas sled and didn't wish to play at this time. However, I was a bit jittery about attempting that precarious toboggan ride down the icy sidewalk and so I hesitatingly led the Snow Bird up the walk and joined Bobby and Katy, Both of them immediately closed in on me, suddenly

---

[33] Fox and geese is a game of tag played in the wintertime.

117

considering me an outsider in spite of Katy's recent invitation to join in the festivities.

I was dismayed at the changed attitude of these two old friends and I gingerly sat on the Snow Bird with both feet squarely on the slippery walk to prevent the possibility of a wild ride. Bobby, interpreting my preparations for those of escape, told me I wasn't to slide on his sidewalk and instructed Katy to get her sled and block my getaway route down the hill. Bobby further explained to me that he was going to salt the walk and did not want anyone to slide on it. Katy maneuvered the family sled (a pitiful, home made, hand sawed barge, minus paint and with only one strap runner) across my prospected course of exit. Bobby, in addition, further blocked my escape by standing in front of my sled and leaning menacingly on an old broom.

I appealed to Bobby. Katy had invited me to come and play. Why now were they both being so unfriendly? I got no response other than a tightening of the guard and a more menacing scowl on the faces of my two captors.

Then Bert appeared at the foot of the hill. He stood precariously on the two stone block steps which raised the Liberty Street sidewalk, (Osmer' side) up to the Sixteenth Street level, the Snow King was at his feet. He beckoned for me to come on down. I called to him (probably in tears) that Bobby and Katy would not let me go.

Bert had, by now, dragged his sled up the steps and stood straddling it with his arms akimbo. He shouted to me to come on down anyway. "Nobody is going to stop you." There was no threat nor challenge in his voice, just a simple order which I was loath to disobey.

The effect of his order on my keepers was electrifying. Katy pulled the ugly wooden sled to the side of the walk. Bobby dropped his broom and retreated backwards just one step, caught his heel in the heavy snow and sat unceremoniously on the snow covered terrace at the foot of the big lilac bush. My right of way was now free of all encumbrances. I arose from my sitting position on the Snow Bird and throwing all caution aside, made one leap at the sled and went careening down that treacherous walk belly buster. All fear of the consequences of my daring were gone.

I slithered down that slippery, narrow runway at ever increasing velocity, whistled past Mom Bridge's ornamental iron fence at unheard of speed (to me) started braking at the corner, where Bert stood, but feeling no slowing effect, I eased up on my trailing feet and concentrated on keeping myself and Snow Bird on the straight and narrow. I assume that I shot by Bert, who had undoubtedly seen me careening blindly toward him. He must have stepped aside. We went past my house like a rocket. The two wooden "up steps" at the Barnes' house, where the stone slab walk ended and the wooden walk began were completely covered by a bank of snow.

Of course during any of the last five seconds of this frightening race, I could have dragged my left foot harder and steered into the snowed-under two foot terrace and thus brought the whole ride to a conclusion. But I was only a small boy and I was far too excited to reason. If someone had had the gumption to sweep the snow off of that walk way, just past the Riesenman house, where there was an empty lot, I don't believe there would have been enough left of me to sop up in a bucket. But, in a daze, I did drag feet vigorously as I saw those snow covered, wooden steps approaching, loosened my grip on the hand rail and thus was pulled clear of the sled allowing it to finish that wild ride alone. I slid on my face and chest for the last thirty feet and due to the heavy snow, ended up as a white ball directly behind Snow Bird. I untangled myself from my arms and legs, searched out the pull rope to the sled and, after dusting the snow from my clothes, limpingly retraced my way towards home.

Bert arrived a few seconds later and, after surveying my snow filled face, remarked that Bobby and Katy were just envious of my new sled and had blocked my departure for that reason.

I'll never forget how grateful I was of Bert's understanding of my predicament. Nor his shouted instructions to me, in a commanding voice, That I was to come on down, "They wont stop you!"

WHO WANTS TO BE A FIREMAN?
(Circa 1902-1903)

And then there was the time when brother Bert and I had just gotten out of bed and were engaged in a contest to determine which of us could dress the faster. 1 was leading by a shirt and one pants leg. I reached for my stockings, and could only find one. A search under the bed covers revealed the other one and I immediately accused Bert of having hidden it there so that he could win. This, he denied. quite an alteration ensued and big brother P.W., from the sanctity of his own bed room, called and asked what was the trouble.

An explanation by me that I would have broken a fireman's record for quick dressing except that Bert had hidden one of my stockings, brought a lusty guffaw from brother P.W. He closed the interview, I closed the door.

What had I done that I should be burdened by having two such uncooperative brothers? One who imperiled my chances of breaking a record by hiding my stocking at a crucial moment. The other who had openly laughed at me for having the temerity to announce that I had almost broken such a record. A few moments of reflection reminded me that maybe I was at fault. That, undoubtedly, I was the late comer, the imposter, that my brothers had both been around prior to the time that I was even thought of. Anyhow they were taking advantage of me and I didn't appreciate it.

About five minutes later, P.W. called to me sleepily and again laughed at my assertion about setting a record. He seemed to be half asleep and the bed covers were pulled up to his neck. He told me that if I would go back into my bedroom, shut the door and start counting, he would set a record for me to shoot at. I complied and had not completely closed the door, much less started counting, when he called "OK Pug come in." There he sat on the side of his bed completely dressed, stooped over and apparently finishing the tying of his second shoe.

120

Amazing, astounding, impossible, this feat of dressing in zero seconds was beyond comprehension. It had taken him no longer to find his clothes, put them on and be ready for inspection than it would for me to throw the covers back and swing out of bed.

The idea that he would practice perfidy and be deceitful to his little brother never entered my sharp mind. Well, not for a few years, anyhow.

THE YELLOW FIRECRACKER
(Circa 1902-1903)

And then there was the time when, (right after breakfast, on the Fourth of July, to be exact) Bert and I were conservatively shooting firecrackers in our side yard. We would scrape a little cavity in the grassy terrace on the Riesenman side of our lawn, drop a firecracker into the depression, cover up all except the fuse which was then touched with the hot end of a piece of glowing punk[34]. The resulting explosion was muffled and mild but it did throw a fist full of dirt into the air and was quite entertaining.

Bert would always assemble quite a few firecrackers of various sizes and store them in a shoe box several days before the Fourth. The contents of this box was carefully guarded by my brother, but special privileges were occasionally granted to me and I was allowed to look, but not to touch, these treasures with Bert standing at my side, holding the open box in one hand and the lid in the other. The box usually contained eight to ten nickel packs of crackers which were purchased from the Chinese laundryman at his place of business on Liberty Street. Assortment of snakes-in-the-grass and two or three whistling cannon crackers with those curling barber pole stripes in red, white and blue. And then always present in Bert's shoe box, the one monster ten inch cracker, about the size of a flashlight of present day vintage – it's boom to announce the end of that fabulous celebration as contained in the pasteboard box.

The mysterious William Lewis appeared from nowhere and sat on the terrace beside me. Our house was definitely not his stamping ground. You know he was the boy whose father told him that Harry Kellar had sold his soul to the devil and was thereby able to perform impossible feats of magic. I welcomed him, not forgetting to address him properly as William and I introduced him to Bert. He grunted in

---

[34] A prepared substance, usually in stick form, that will smolder and can be used to light fireworks, fuses, etc.

122

response to Bert's cheerful hello and sat there beside him, watching longingly as we continued to explode firecrackers muffled in the turf.

Bert noticed that our visitor was not shooting any firecrackers and inquired if he (William) had not had any at all. "Yep," says William, "I already shot 'em all – three packs." It must have been the plaintiveness of his reply or the ragged shirt which he was wearing, because I felt an overpowering surge of pity and compassion for this poor fellow creature who had had only three packs of crackers with which to celebrate the glorious Fourth. Silly me. I do think that tears were in my eyes when I conferred with my brother with the idea of maybe allowing my guest to have, at least a part of a pack from Bert's vast storeroom.

"Well Jim I don't see why you should feel sorry for him. You only had two packs yourself." This was undeniably true - but I returned and sat down beside William, reached in my pocket, procured three loose firecrackers, with the firm determination of giving two of them to my visitor.

I suggested to Bert that he let William see inside that shoebox and Bert condescendingly removed the lid and let my friend have a look - not touch - the treasures which the box contained. Now among those packages of Chinese crackers, which were predominantly red, there were always a couple of green ones and a yellow one; perhaps to lend a touch of variety to the appearance of the pack. These different colored ones went off with the same loud bang as the red ones but I always saved the yellow cracker until the last, just one of my childish customs, I guess.

"Gimme the loan of your squib!" demanded William, referring to my three inch stick of smoldering punk. He immediately broke it into two pieces and lighted the longer piece by pushing the hot end of the other one onto it and blowing vociferously at the junction. He didn't return the larger piece to me, as I had expected, but held both of them in his left hand – reached over and grabbed my three crackers, two red and one yellow, from my hand, outstretched to receive the expected return of at least one piece of the borrowed punk. I didn't like his attitude and

123

suggested that he return, at least, the yellow cracker to me. He ignored my pleading, twisted the fuses of those three together, lighted them and tossed them into my lap.

I was furious, as I jumped to my feet, brushing those three sputtering explosives from my lap. This was a quality in William, the quiet reserved boy, of my acquaintance, which I had never observed before. I had never been noted for my ability as a pugilist[35] although I was frequently addressed as "Pug" - a name which I had acquired, not because of my pugilistic ability, but rather on account of the blunt contour of my "schnoz." I never did like contests in which bodily contact was a prime requisite, this included boxing. Really, if a professional nickname maker had been called into service, I surely would have been given the name of the color of the firecracker about which this episode has been written.

Source of nickname notwithstanding, I blew up mentally as that special yellow firecracker went off at my feet. I lunged at William with the ferocity of a tiger and sent him sprawling backwards down that terrace. He was bigger than I was but I was mad and then too, Bert was there to take my part if William reacted in any wise other than the gentleman which I had, up toll now, thought him to be. But William regained his feet and, much to my astonishment, ran like a scared rabbit, down our driveway and out into Sixteenth Street. I didn't follow him even with my eyes, but he was probably more frightened than I was and sought the sanctuary of his home grounds.

Suppose, according to Bert's theory, William was filled with envy when he was given that fleeting glance at the contents of that cardboard shoe box. Yes I was a bit jealous of Bert myself.

---

[35] A boxer, especially a professional one.

CINCINNATI, OHIO

AND THIS ONE TOO IS TRUE
(Circa 1910 – 1915)

Before the days of cubists in futuristic artists, the picture of a wooded hillside looked like a wooded hillside. A reproduction on canvas of the setting sun appeared to be a picture of the setting sun. That was before the advent of the early 20th century impressionists, and that is when this little drama of the quiet, peaceful, sensible life took place.

My Brother Bert and I hesitated for a few seconds before ringing the front doorbell of Aunt Clara's and Uncle Will's cramped little brick dwelling. We had been invited to visit them, on this, our second day of a three day vacation in Philadelphia, have a cup of tea, a cookie and, as a special privilege, allotted only to the family in a few favored patrons, we were to have the opportunity of viewing Uncle Will's latest artistic creation.

Clara, a sweet, chubby, motherly girl of 70, greeted us warmly at the door. But before inviting us to come inside, she confided in us that tea had a tendency to upset Will's stomach and disposition. She further disclosed that if we could make our appearance bearing a bottle of ale, it would be most gratifying to Will and help put him in a mood of friendship and camaraderie towards us. She further disclosed that the little delicatessen just a block north on Howard Street, always kept a supply of Ganet's Ale on ice. Conveniently too, Ganet's Ale which was Will's favored soothing lotion was put up in quart bottles, which by chance, was Will's favored size. And then, inasmuch as we were determined to walk to the delicatessen shop anyhow, why not fetch two bottles? Will could have the second one later in the day.

Uncle Will was a dreamer, an artistic dreamer who considered himself a reincarnation of Michelangelo, da Vinci or Rubens. The Dutchman Vincent Van Gogh, who departed this life when Will was about 20 years of age, was considered by our illustrious uncle, as a brazen young upstart and not worthy of emulation. Will was two visionary, temperamental and devoted to the arts to allow himself to

127

consider being swallowed in any of the vast commercial opportunities of his time, for he would thus deny to cultured mankind, the products of his great creative ability.

Mr. Colson, the haberdasher[36], had offered Will part time employment clerking in the store and the Germantown National Bank and Trust Company president, Mr. Shamert, had made it known to Clara that her husband might, if he chose, preside over a proposed customer information desk, which could be set up in the lobby of the bank. Offers of both of these dignified positions have been promoted, not through need of the employer or his business, but the cause of friendship for Charlie, the only son of Will and Clara. Cousin Charlie was a rather successful traveling representative of the Prudential Insurance Company and had acquired the knack of making many close friends. Charlie's beneficence was responsible for the neat little nest in which his parents resided, and also he mailed to Clara, a semimonthly check for household expenses. Everyone who knew Charlie liked him, everyone who knew Clara loved her and everyone who knew Will tolerated him because of his relationship to Clara and Charlie.

On several occasions, Will had reluctantly parted with one of his fabulous paintings. I remember when my mother pressed three ten-spots[37] into Clara's hand, declaring that she would "just die" if she couldn't only the twelve by eighteen canvas of Will's: a blob of green and white paint, presumably depicting an expanse of turbulent sea with a tiny disabled schooner in the very, very far distance. Will was loath to part with this masterpiece, but Clara coyly waved the three ten-spots in his direction and pleaded that Alice, of his very own family, could be trusted to make the picture happy in her home and that the picture, in turn, would make Alice happy.

These infrequent sales of Will's artistry were always, of necessity, made to relatives or close friends and were always engineered by Clara, and invariably seemed to be consummated at a time when a

---

[36] A dealer in men's clothing.
[37] Slang. A ten-dollar bill.

128

bit of extra cash was needed for canvas, paints, brushes or ale, the consumption of which was the only apparent physical vice which Will entertained.

Bert and I again presented ourselves at Aunt Clara's door and after handing over the two cold Ganet bottles, we were ushered into the presence of the august and talented personage, a master of the arts, the dreamer of miracles, but otherwise a rather lazy and cranky old conniver. That was Uncle Will. He greeted us cordially, having been tipped off by Clara that we came bearing gifts particularly brewed to his liking.

Clara produced a pot of tea and several spice cakes from a secret room at the end of a long hallway and we, Clara, my brother and I, sat in three most uncomfortable, straight back chairs in one corner of the parlor. We attempted to carry on what must've been a decidedly stilted conversation. Yet dear old Clara was jovial and asked questions and told us of some of the magnificent more recent accomplishments of our gifted Uncle. Will, for his contribution to the gaiety of the occasion, had taken refuge in another part of the room, in the only upholstered chair of which this home could boast. He had been supplied by Clara with a little black tin tray on which rested one of the two bottles of ale, and in his hand he clinched a ruby red tumbler, overflowing with that foamy, soothing ale.

There followed about ten minutes of questions and answers, none of which contributed to our scintillating, nor to Bert and me, interesting conversation. For our part, we were making, at Clara's request, a courtesy call. We have but little in common with dear Aunt Clara. In fact, we lived in Cincinnati and Clara's home was in Germantown, a Philadelphia suburb, So geographically, as well as temperamentally, we were miles apart. Suddenly we realize that the great moment had, at last, arrived.

Will handed the tin tray, ruby glass an empty bottle to Clara, arose and with a slow but elegance sweep of his arms, opened the portieres,[38] which served as a door to the adjoining room where his easel was standing, draped in a baby blue, summer weight blanket. This room was the master's studio, really the dining room, but the little dinner table had been pushed back, out of the way and the four dining chairs were lined up against one wall, the seats covered with newspaper on which rested Will's tools of trade, brushes, paints, a palate, a knife and paint covered smear-cloth. Meals were of little consequence, especially if they interfere with the arts - in this household Will's works took priority over all domestic activities.

Bert and I were ushered into this sacred chamber. Will carefully positioned us facing the blue blanket. He meticulously adjusted the shade of the little window to admit just the exact amount of light for perfect viewing, and then as Clara inquired, "Are you ready boys?" Will, with a great flourish, threw back the blanket from the square of canvas which it had concealed.

As we gazed in wonder at the work of art, a dead silence fell over that little assembly. My own reaction was uncertain. I didn't know whether to appear awed by the magnificence of the painting and offer an amazed "Oh-h-h" as my contribution to my Uncle's prowess, or to accept the picture in a lighter spirit and audibly giggle. I did neither.

This expanse of canvass depicted in dirty brown, what I assumed to be, a flat, sandy beach. At the far right was plastered an equally extensive covering of sickly green paint, threaded with a few jagged stripes of white - this undoubtedly represented the treacherous sea. Yes, there in the very, very remote distance was a little black daub, probably a sinking and abandon schooner. All of Will's pictures had a ship of some sort in the distance, whether there was water represented or not. On the edge of the brown smear, where it touched the sickly green of the sea, rested three very large and slightly burned meatballs, which, Clara let it be known were rocks left by a passing glacier. Oh, of course the upper half of the picture was filled with the usual crags and peaks of

---

[38] A curtain hung in a doorway, either to replace the door or for decoration.

distant hills, many telltale, saw tooth blots of hazy light blue. The smears we understandingly accepted as a faraway mountain range.

Bert and I stood spellbound and silent as we viewed this amazing masterpiece. The silence was almost audible as I groped for something to say. I prayed that my big brother would exercise the prerogative of an elder brother and come up with some appropriate quip, suggestion, or complimentary statement to break the tenseness of the situation. Bert, I reasoned, in spite of his more mature age and experience, must have been as stupefied as myself as he made no comment. I then discerned, from glancing at my big brother, that he was no less concerned with making the proper remarks of praise for the merits of the painting than he was with the mental insecurity of dear old Aunt Clara who was tense and nervous and in her dire anxiety hoped against hope that one or the other of us would utter some sage saying which would be in praise of the artwork, and would not be offensive to her spouse. For Clara had been the hapless intermediary between Will and his selective clientele in many previous first viewings. She was an experienced and usually silent but apprehensive guardian of Will's quick temper.

Will had taken up a viewing at the left hand edge of a canvas, the edge opposite to the meatballs. I glanced at his face, it was stern but expectant. Clara stood behind him, nervously clenching and unclenching her pink little hands. An expression, which could be translated into vanishing hope, was discernible on her customarily smiling, sweet countenance. This look, doubtless, was what restrained Bert from venturing an opinion about the painting.

The silence became unbearable and finally, in desperation, I blurted out the most vivid white lie of my youth. "Uncle Will that's as beautiful as nature." - If the previous tension had been at the breaking point, the next ten seconds of it screamed in torture. Bert looked relieved, but tears appeared in Clara's eyes and she dabbed at her face with a frilly little lace square of handkerchief.

But as for Will, his face became livid, his eyes glared wildly and as he threw that little baby blue blanket back over the masterpiece, he

131

shouted in a shrill and disdainful voice, "Young man it is more beautiful than nature," and immediately cut me to pieces with a sharp, glinting eye. I'll never forget that look of contempt that he leveled at me - my stupidity was apparently beyond comprehension.

Bert and I managed to conclude our visit without suffering bodily harm. Will, with Clara's help, shooed us out of the studio, closed the portieres, stamped viciously down the hall, out of sight and out of our lives.

Dear, sweet, round Aunt Clara was shedding copious tears when we made our departure. Intermingled with her sniffles was her halfhearted request that we return soon. Then she waived from the doorway a hurried goodbye and probably hastened to Uncle Will to comfort him in his mortification and sorrow and having two such stupid nephews.

Bert and I, thanks partially to geographical distance, never visited this home again. In fact we never again found it necessary to cater to the whims of this relative who was so pompous and prideful that he considered his own prowess superior to that of the deity.

THE CHINESE JOURNALIST
(Circa 1904)

And then there was the time when I was in the fourth grade of the Sixteenth Intermediate School and I had been intrigued by the strange characters on the little wrappers that each enclosed a one and one half inch cube of gift tea. Two of these little packages had been given to my mother as a going away present by our Chinese laundryman just before we moved from Franklin to Cincinnati. In a moment of constructive idleness, I had copied several of those funny red ink scribblings on a sheet of tablet paper and taken the sheet to school for further study.

Arthur Smith was a classmate of mine. He was a slim white haired boy who invariably wore a small tight fitting coat of dead black with knee pants to match. His spit white collar was celluloid[39] and he wore with it a little dead black pre-tied bow tie which was more or less firmly affixed to the brassy gold collar button that protruded from the flaps of the celluloid collar. Smitty's demeanor was solemn and his deportment was as good as my own - practically perfect. All things considered he might grow up to develop into a first class mortician.

Arthur saw me studying my copy of the tea wrapper and questioned me on my knowledge of the Chinese language. Although I denied being able to either write or speak Chinese fluently, I must have given the impression that I was well versed in the subject.

"George," he begged, "write the Chinese alphabet for me, will ya?"

---

[39] Celluloid is a thermoplastic, registered in 1870. Celluloid is easily molded and shaped. It was widely used as an ivory replacement for photographic film, table tennis balls,, and detachable shirt collars and cuffs. A detachable shirt collar made of Celluloid could be wiped clean with a damp rag and thus extend the time between shirt washings.

"Smitty," says I, "the Chinese don't have an alphabet. A rather hazy bit of information which I had picked up from somewhere in the past, probably from my Port Hope educated brother.

"Oh come on George," pleaded the future undertaker, "I won't tell no one. Willie Seerard, resident of the orphan's home on Auburn Avenue and my ally and personal protector intervened. "George says they ain't got no alphabet, so leave him be." This admonition from Willie put a temporary halt to the alphabet question.

That afternoon, at home, I decided that if Smitty was so anxious to learn Chinese, I was not the one to deny him the privilege. So I began laboriously to print for him my own version of the Oriental's alphabet. I grew tired of the effort after completing the first nine letters and to round things out I completed the work with the X the Y and the Z.

My version of the oriental man's key to literature was duly presented to Arthur on the next school day. It looked something like this:

$$\tilde{a} \; \textit{ль} \; \dot{c} \text{ etc. ending with } \chi \; \lambda \; \text{ь}.$$

Smitty was enthralled with this gift, and during that morning's reading class in Miss Molly Carroll's room, he busied himself with writing his name in the new, revised Chinese. He questioned me while loud mouthed Martha Miller was struggling through a rendition of the "Village Blacksmith" from her reader. "P-s-s-s-t, George I got started pretty good, I've got the A in Arthur and the I and H in Smith, but what about those missing letters?"

"Oh," I whispered, suddenly inspired, "You fill in the missing letter with these." and I marked a tic-tac-toe playing field on his proffered scribble sheet. After the reading lesson came recess and I went out to play, leaving Smitty alone to print his name in Chinese.

When I returned, Smitty showed me the results of his endeavor. Looked something like this:

$$\tilde{a} \; \# \; \# \; \hbar \; \# \; \# \; \# \; \# \; \ddot{\imath} \; \# \; \hbar$$

134

Arthur didn't return to school that year, fact is I never saw him again. One of our mutual friends reported to me that Arthur's father, with his family, had been transferred to San Francisco.

Many years later, I learned, from the same mutual friend, he was working in Chinatown as a copy boy for one of the many little publications of that area. He was paid five dollars a week, pretty good pay for a young man in those days. No doubt his keen knowledge of the Chinese language had started him on a lucrative literary career. At least I like to think that my instruction in primitive Chinese was partially responsible for his success in this field instead of the mortuary job for which, we all thought, he was best suited.

TO CINCINNATI YET?
(Circa 1905)

And then there was the time when I was in the fifth grade of the 16th district school - Miss Cunningham presiding - a clamor arose in the schoolyard directly below our windows and Nelly Climer, whose desk was on that side of the room, looked out one of the windows and then whispered in a voice which could be heard throughout the class, "Anna, I think it's your baby brother."

This brought an immediate response from Anna Monahan. She rushed to a window, reached over the wooden drafts screen and raise the sash, "Morgan" she shrieked in a shrill staccato voice, "Morgan! you go right home to your mother, Morgan, this minute, you hear me?"

There was little doubt but what Morgan heard her. Everybody within a mile heard her. The other members of the class scrambled to their feet and rushed to see. Morgan, a four year old boy, and his buddies, three or four in number who were causing the original commotion in the yard, were all looking skyward. "Look sis," called Morgan, pointing towards the sky, "a bloon!"

Miss Cunningham, whose classroom was directly across the hall from the principal's office, was definitely embarrassed as she tried vainly to restore order. Then, Mr. Haywood himself appeared in the doorway. The class suddenly regained its composure as Mr. Heywood stumped across the room and looked out the window. Then turning to the teacher and pulling his watch from his vest pocket, he addressed her, "I think Miss Cunningham, that all of the children will profit by seeing the airship and as it is just five minutes to twelve, I am going to ring the dismissal bell."

The bell clanged in the hallways and about six hundred excited students marched out of their classrooms, boys to the north, girls to the south. All immediately search the skies for a glimpse of the "bloon." Word got around quickly in those days. A small cigar shaped airship was hovering about a quarter mile above the school building and two little figures (the crew) were plainly visible perched on the scaffold like frame which hung beneath the cigar.

As we watched, the ship circled once and then began a slow descent, but it also traveled in an easterly direction. It was undoubtedly going to land, but where? Most of the children lost interest and hastened home to lunch. I jogged for home, and as home was in the direction of the airship's departure - I might get to see it again at closer range. When I reached the corner of Nelson and McGregor, (the Krehbiel and Wilson corner) a group of about 20 boys from school were already there in the vacant lot just above Mary Louise Wilson's home and there too was the airship, it's gasbag caught in a grove of scrub trees, but it's flimsy frame was resting, quite comfortable, on that rocky and weed grown hillside lot.

Two very thin man had already alighted and while one of them was attempting to free the partially deflated and distorted bag from the trees, the other had gone into the Wilson house, presumably to call on the phone for his ground crew. Having no further business there, I proceeded towards home. As I left, school boys who were gathered, hopefully to see the landing of those two noble aeronauts, gave three lusty cheers for them. Although, only one member of the crew was present at cheer time. I believed, at the time, that this outburst of acclaim was rather stupid and I continued on home.

About one half hour later, on my way back to school for the afternoon session, as I came to Mary Louise's corner, a big two-horse van with a long flatbed trailer was standing at the curb. The cigar-shaped balloon had apparently been completely deflated and stored in the van by that prompt and alert ground crew. One half of the (shall I call it fuselage) was in the process of being laid on the trailer. This gave me an opportunity to study the other half of that flimsy structure, which was lying on the sidewalk.

It consisted of four bamboo poles, each about ten or twelve feet in length with one foot bamboo spacers wired into them, forming a boxlike frame. The half of this frame, which still lay on the sidewalk and which I was able to study closely, was the after or stern section. A bicycle saddle was strapped to it at the rear end. The saddle faced the bow of the ship and a tiny gasoline engine, similar to that of the Orient Buckboard's [40] power plant was connected to a little, wooden two-bladed propeller by way of a length of one-half inch galvanized pipe which acted as a driveshaft. The front half of the frame had already been loaded on the flat bed trailer. It too had a saddle fastened to it - facing backwards - it's occupant looking toward the miniature and untrustworthy engine for the purpose, I assumed, of being in better position when the engine stopped, of aiming his prayers or epithets at it. The rudder was a little square of canvas tacked to a bamboo frame and was controlled by two pieces of clothes line tied to opposite ends of a section of broomstick which the rear aviator undoubtedly held across his lap, his arms extended. The forward and rear halves of this flimsy frame had been connected by, of all things, friction tape,[41] wrapped innumerable times around the protruding ends of the four bamboo poles. The tape had been cut with a knife for dismantling.

As I looked in amazement at the construction of this frail craft, I came to the conclusion that perhaps I have been remiss in not joining the cheers which my schoolmates they given those two intrepid aviators. They had risked their lives far above the ground, without benefit of parachute in this hit or miss unstable, wickerwork contraption. And now they were having it hauled away in order to repeat this hazardous adventure.

---

[40] The Orient Buckboard was an American automobile built from 1903 until 1908.

[41] As used in this context, friction tape is one of the oldest known electrical tapes. It was designed to replace the cotton jacketing used in early cable and wire assemblies. It is a simple construction of cotton cloth impregnated with a tacky, rubber compound that provides good adhesion to all types of surfaces.

THAT GREAT CAMMAMALER CAKE
(Circa 1911-1912)

And then there was the time when I was interested in athletics at Hughes High School in Cincinnati, and we (the junior and senior classes) were having an afternoon get-together in our beautiful new gymnasium - fact is, the whole building was beautiful, and only a year old.[42] The captaincy of the track team had just been wished on me. I wasn't elected to this position because of any outstanding athletic ability nor because I was the physical director's pet. It was just that only a few of my classmates were interested enough in track and field events to put extra time into their promotion.

And so I was asked to arrange for fifteen minutes of my team's time to show off their agility before the serious dancing began. Although I was "hard put" to find a good excuse for trying to entertain the student body, as well as the attending faculty, with track-suited boys, jumping or running top speed around the elliptical track, I was finally blessed with an idea. After fiddling for some time with just what to call it, something mysterious and yet never before heard of, I settled on the word "Cammamaler."

My mother helped by ordering a huge cocoanut cake from White's bakery, had them splash that silly word cammamaler across it's top in pink icing, and she even cooperated to the extent of making a special trip into town to carry that big piece of confectionery back home. The cake was to be offered as first prize in the quarter mile, timed race among my contemporaries. Advance advertising was essential to build up interest and I did that by visiting many of the classrooms before and after school hours and chalking on their blackboards the slogan – "See the great Cammamaler cake race." – (in the gym next Friday p.m.) All of these adds were signed "by George," and my simple cartooned head of "George" was always present.

---

[42] Hughes Highs School was completed in 1910.

Enough to say that the advertising campaign built up more interest among my classmates than the race itself, which was won by Irving Powers, a fine young unselfish Jewish boy.

A three piece band was there to supply music for dancing: Sam Montague at the piano, Allan Burns on drums, both of whom were members of my class. But the third instrument, a violin, was played by a "ringer" whom I had never seen before. Later, I heard that he was a semi-professional, and that Carrie Perrin, our French teacher, had arranged for his appearance - even paid him two dollars out of her own pocket - just for a few squeaks on the violin.

The dancing was slow to materialize and Mr. King, my home room teacher with the help of Mr. Cook, another professor, tried to get things started by appearing on the floor in front of the temporary band stand and going through the sad routine of an Irish jig, then they tried a sailor's hornpipe. The were both rather short and fat and this effort was exhausting but also unappreciated. Something had to be done or the whole afternoon would flop completely. Then, Sam Montague suggested to Mr. Cook that he do a cake walk[43] for the delectation of the wallflowers. Irving Powers who now was the rightful owner of the Great Cammamaler Cake, dropped his option and offered it as the prize to the best cake walk team. Mr. Cook tried vainly for some time to interest a girl student, any girl student in becoming his cake walk partner and thereby making a spectacle of herself. Finally, Felicia Frank, a junior bit of flouncy feminine vitality, entered the area and amid a burst of hand clapping, spiced with giggles, she pirouetted onto front stage grasped Mr. Cook's extended hand and while the piano, fiddle and drums struck up an appropriate tune, she and Mr. Cook went into a classical version of a cake walk. Mr. king, not to be outdone, grabbed Carrie Perrin and bent over backwards so far that his bald head almost touched the floor, and these two cake walkers joined in the competition.

---

[43] A circular procession of couples who walked in their very best manner around the room before judges, who selected the best turned-out pair, and presented them with a cake.

I have never before, nor since seen such a laughable display of comic Terpsichore[44] as these two round and fat pedagogues,[45] accompanied by their partners put on.

These two teams were the only contestants, but they both tried feverishly to out do and out perform the opposition. Legs flying, skirts swishing, both men teachers bending over backwards to the extent that we all wondered how they kept their balance. Mr. Fezziwig[46] dancing at his own ball in the story of David Copperfield might have been a fair comparison to the gyrations of these four fervent strutters.

Then Mr. King, feeling the exuberance of youth, grabbed the cake from the top of the piano, where it had been placed, held it high on the fingers of his right hand, much like an experienced waiter does in carrying a tray of food through a crowded restaurant. He leaned back a trifle too far. His heel must have contacted a damp spot on the gymnasium floor, for, up went the cake, down went King, immediately to be joined by the returning cake right on his little fat stomach.

The embarrassed professor was helped to his feet, mopped off by his fellow teachers and retired from further competition. - Oh, that Cake? Although it landed face down on the soft belly of the King, it broke and splattered in many directions. Someone got a push broom and hastened it's remains under the bandstand.

And then the ice, as well as the cake, having been broken, the dancing took up in earnest. I, for one, believe that "The Great Cammamaler Cake" was a success, not in the way I had anticipated, but a success never the less.

---

[44] The Greek Muse of dancing and choral song.
[45] Meaning teachers.
[46]Fezziwig is a character in Charles Dickens' *A Christmas Carol* not *David Copperfield*.

"DEMYUM"[47] TAKES US FOR A SPIN
(Circa 1904 -1906)

And then there was the time when Bert and I were back in Franklin for a few weeks after having moved to Cincinnati. We were paying guests at our old house, now Huntington's, and had been invited to dinner at Grants.

Parked in the port-cochère [48] of the Grant's home was a magnificent, new Stoddard Dayton touring car, all shiny and black. After dinner, Mrs. Grant in her high pitched but somewhat garbled voice, suggested that maybe we boys would like to take a ride in the "cah." "I'm sure Dennison will be glad to drive and Harry will go with you." I referred to Mrs. Grant's voice as high pitched and garbled. Imagine, if you can, the voice of the late Mrs. F.D.R.[49] now plop a handful of keyster[50] sized marbles into her mouth and let her continue to talk. And there you have an exact reproduction of Mrs. Grant's voice, as I remember it.

Harry lighted and adjusted the acetylene head lamps, arranged the spark and throttle levers on the steering wheel and cranked the engine. "Grinny" Read wandered into our midst when we were getting into the car and he was politely invited by "Demyum" to join us. the Stoddard Dayton's engine burst into a healthy roar due to Harry's liberal starting setting of the hand throttle on the wheel and this setting was allowed to remain throughout our trip. Fortunately, the driver left the low gear engaged as we rolled out of the driveway and turned down Liberty Street. Otherwise, the tour would have ended abruptly on one of

---

[47] In a hand written footnote in the original text, GHS II explains that "Demyum" was Grinny Reed's attempt to pronounce "Dennison"

48 A port-cochère, coach gate or carriage porch is a porch-or portico-like structure at a main or secondary entrance to a building through which a horse and carriage (or motor vehicle) can pass in order for the occupants to alight under cover, protected from the weather.

[49] Franklin Delano Roosevelt, 32nd President of the Unites States.

[50] Most likely "keister," a suitcase, bag, or box for carrying possessions or merchandise.

those big trees which were set in the tree lawn on the left hand side of the road. For Denny, who couldn't have possibly been more than twelve years old, favored the left hand side of all streets and did most of maneuvering with the wheel, to the exclusion of brakes and throttle.

We zoomed down the Liberty Street hill at a high rate of speed, in spite of the fact that the car was in first gear. As we approached Thirteenth Street, we veered to the right-hand corner as our pilot steered the heavy car abruptly to the left to go north on Thirteenth Street. We slurred around the corner on not more than two wheels. This sudden ninety degree turn was probably the result of the military training of Denny's father, who demanded that a right angle turn when marching was to be precisely executed, pivoting on the inside heel and swinging the opposite leg completely around to the new direction in continuous movement.

I wondered why brother Harry didn't suggest that the driver switch to a higher gear and close the throttle control. Concluded that Harry was as untutored in car operation as was our driver. Yet Harry had lighted the kerosene tail lamp, gas headlights and had cranked the engine without disastrous results.

We barreled along Thirteenth Street, still careening on the left-hand side of the street. Fortunately, there was no traffic to impede our progress and we sped onto the little iron bridge across French Creek, on up the hill and across the Erie Railroad tracks, we were again hurled into the right-hand corner of the seat as Denny made another military turn to the left.

Something finally occurred to the driver and with a great clash of gears he managed to shift the car into second speed. We roared out the road paralleling the Erie tracks for some distance, perhaps a mile or two. How we got turned around on that narrow road was still a mystery to me, but we did. Probably that helpful boost from a well placed pole, enabling the car to stop before going into a ditch, was instrumental in our turn. That lovely Stoddard Dayton engine was roaring in protest all through this maneuver. We rushed along the same road from which we had approached.

Then a car's lights appeared in the distance coming toward us. I held my breath, as we were still following the driver's practice of sticking closely to the left-hand side of the highway. At this time, I realized that Denny's religion would not permit of anyone being hurt. I didn't know what the theory of the Christian Scientists was on being killed.

We passed the other car in a flurry of dust and a definite clash of hub caps or running boards or both. But Denny was adamant and kept on going, remarking, in an undertone, that the driver of the other car should be more careful. At this point I closed my eyes and kept them closed for the remainder of the excursion. I could tell when we turned to the right by the fact that "Grinny" and I were twice tumbled into Bert's lap - once turning into the bridge road and again into Liberty Street. Opening my eyes again when we finally came to a stop under Grant's port-cochère. The car's radiator was boiling violently, due to Denny's favoritism for low and second gear and for the high throttle setting which had never been reduced.

I hastened to leave, not even taking time to examine the left side of the car to determine what damage had been done. But was I thankful to be able to walk away! Immediately concluded that the Grant family would be better off and live longer if they stuck to horses.

LET'S TRY CINCINNATI AGAIN
(Circa 1903 -1912)

And then there was the time when we, Mrs. Duttenhofer her son Clifford, our mother, Bert and I and John Wessell, the Duttenhofer chauffeur, had been riding along the countryside near Cincinnati. We had stopped at the farm home of the amiable widow Annie Blunk and her old maid sister Sally. Our purpose was to get a drink of cold water from the well, also to buy a couple "fresh eggs from Annie, the happy widow.

On this visit, Annie was her usual buoyant self, but old maid distrustful sister Sally Jackson with her witchlike attitude had retreated to the kitchen and could be seen, from time to time, peering into the parlor through a half opened door. It was almost beyond reason that these two distinctly opposite personalities could be blood relatives. But Sally was "tetched" in the head and was not responsible for all of her odd endeavors.

Poor old sister Sally, although she had immediately retreated to the kitchen when Mrs. Duttenhofer and Mother were greeted with animation by Annie, had evidently heard the request for eggs, and had managed to keep out of sight and refrained from being cordial to her visitors, she had packed two dozen eggs in a paper sack. Now, evidently in order to speed the guests on their way, she opened wide the door from the kitchen and tossed the egg-filled sack at an upholstered chair in the parlor, exclaiming in her harsh witches voice, "There's them eggs Annie, two dozen." The sack missed the chair and fell with a dull thud on the wood floor.

Annie, undaunted, retrieved the sack and attempted to salvage the unbroken eggs from that packaged omelet, laughingly called to her sister, "Oh Sally you shouldn't a did that, them's the last eggs we got." Needless to say if the sack of eggs had, perchance, found their destination on the chair, most of them would have broken anyhow. Mrs. Duttenhofer insisted on paying Annie the full purchase price of twenty five cents anyhow, although not a single egg had survived the crash. Annie's search of the chicken house revealed not one more egg, she smilingly suggested that we visit her brother John, who lived with his wife on the other side of Madeira.

Annie, Sally and fat John were the three remaining members of the Jackson family and Annie was the one who was not handicapped by a lack of brain power or initiative. Annie, before her unfortunate marriage, had made a home for simple-minded Sally and had continued to maintain her after the demise of her, (Annie's) husband. It was also said that Annie found a wife for her inactive brother fat John and thus supplied him with a helpmate who overcame the results of his inability to make a go of anything in his complicated world.

We piled into the Packard and soon were at fat John Jackson's dilapidated farm house. John, the oh-so rotund, oh-so lazy farmer was sitting on a log by the road in front of the farm house. We had often commented on fat John's lack of initiative. His wife did everything that had to be done while John sat around contemplating his next big project. He was even too lazy to whittle while he thought.

As we drove up, fat John didn't leave his log, but with an apparent burst of energy, raised his right hand in a festive greeting. Fat John studied the Packard with an imaginative and critical eye while Mother and our host walked to the house in search of eggs to replace the omelet. Cliff, Bert and I gathered around John's log and conversed with him while John Wessell got out a screwdriver and tightened the hinge on one of the car's doors.

Fat John started the conversation with the casual remark, "I reckon I'll make me one of them things for myself," at the same time gesturing with his thumb toward the Packard. We three boys were speechless. Fat John guessed he had a couple of wheels in the shed, "What would do. It 'ud be handy to go to Georgie's corner in," sez he as he painfully arose and walked over to the car and examined the sleek enamel job on one fender. "Got some paint too," says fat John caressing the fender with his hand.

Through lack of attention to the obvious, John had arrived at the conclusion that an automobile was a simple assemblage of a box mounted on a few wheels, given a coat of paint and it was ready for the road.

While fat John was examining one of the big Deitz headlamps of the car, Bert suggested to John Wessell, in a whisper, that he raise the hood and let fat John see what was underneath. This was done, displaying that massive four cylinder engine, a conglomeration of rods, pipes, copper tubing, rubber covered wiring along with many incidentals, such as the carburetor, governor, heavy brass steering gear box, etc.

Although this early Packard was not redundant with electric starter, air filter, alternator, power steering hydraulic pump, with air conditioner radiator and compressor and other present day accessories which fill the "under hood" cavity to the bursting point, there was a wealth of good, solid, well designed equipment revealed when the bonnet was raised.

Fat John's eyes grew as big as saucers as he gazed at this complex wonder of engineering prowess and clean detail. He stepped back a pace from that Packard, put his thumbs in his overall pockets and dismissed the whole idea with, "Guess I didn't wanna make one nohow."

OTHER ANECDOTES

EARLY INVENTIONS

And then there was the time when I believed that I too could and would become a famous inventor like Thomas Edison. I was told that he and Ben Franklin had invented electricity, but I had also heard that Mr. Franklin broke up this partnership and went into the bakery business in Boston or Philadelphia or somewhere.

The one thing that I was sure of was that Mr. Edison had made, with his own hands, that phonograph which Mary Riesenman sometimes wound up and played on her front porch. This I knew because her phonograph had the name "Edison" written in gold letters right on the front of it's oak case. Mary occasionally would put on the cylinder which played "Fun In The Barnyard" for us kids.

One of my first inventions, or discoveries, was a cardboard razor. Don't you remember how Cracker Jack came in a box for a nickel? Well, in those days the box had an inner lining, it was like a box within a box. The inside box was made of thin yellowish pasteboard which evidently had been treated with wax or oil so that the molasses on the popcorn wouldn't stick to it. Purely by accident, I discovered that when one of the end flaps of this box was torn off and run across my face it sounded exactly like my pop's razor did when he shaved. Lo, I had invented the first safety razor, it predated King C. Gillette's face scraper by two or three years. I didn't call it a safety razor, hadn't thought of that name yet, but it wouldn't cut your face, wouldn't cut whiskers either. But I didn't know that.

The Exchange Barber Shop had a sign in the window, which I was told, read "A fresh towel with every shave." Gosh! I could hardly wait to grow up, start my own barber shop and put a sign in the window, reading "A new razor with every shave." Wouldn't that bring the customers flocking to my shop? Well, I reasoned that at five cents a box, I could save up and buy, perhaps six boxes of Cracker Jack, cut the top flaps off and even cut the whole inner box into half-inch strips and thereby make as many as one hundred blades for the thirty cent investment. Besides I would enjoy eating the contents.

But lets continue on with my second brainy project. Brother Bert and I were amusing ourselves on the back porch. He went into the little refrigerator room at the rear of the porch and closed the door. I, of course, had to snoop, which I promptly did. Bert was perched on top of the icebox with his stockinged legs hanging down in front, kicking his heels against the box. He picked up grains of ice cream salt which he held in his left hand and was apparently popping them into his mouth, one by one. I questioned this procedure, at the same time coming to the conclusion that the salt was a decoy for his real activity – he was mouthing a jawbreaker and didn't want me to hear it clicking on his teeth and subsequently demand one for myself. A jaw breaker was hickory nut size marble of extremely hard candy, made up of layer on layer of alternating white, pink and licorice colored candy, all wrapped around a central anise seed. This delicacy was known to the higher echelons of refined society as a "belly burner." True, those little pill-like red cinnamon drops were also known by this descriptive name, but only by proponents of a lower social order.

So I shouted at Bert and made my desires known for a jaw breaker for myself. This appeal was made in my usual whining yet demanding voice. Bert was not impressed, he jumped down from the icebox, fiddled with the door knob and he removed the knobs from both sides of that door. Went back into his den and closed the door, thereby locking me out. The square in the latch, where the door had been, interested me. I found a piece of wood from the top of a recently opened Macy's box, got the carving knife from the kitchen, and then I split a piece of the box top off and shaved it down to fit that square hole. After a trial fitting, I rammed the squared strip into that metal slot, gave the stick a twist and opened the door, much to Bert's surprise and to mine. Gee, I was proud of my ingenuity, even called Mother to come and see what a clever son she was rearing. My head swelled to the extent that I doubted my ability to walk through the kitchen door to return the knife to it's proper place without losing an ear on the door jamb.

That wooden key scarcely qualifies as an invention but just thought I'd mention it. Now, to another clever symbol of my ever active intellect.

A peanut dropper was a tower made of our most indestructible toys, those little oblong wooden all purpose blocks. They were like miniature bricks made of pine and sanded to splinter-less smoothness. The dropping tower was constructed by alternately laying two of these blocks on edge, parallel, and about two inches apart, putting the next two on top of the first, but at right angles to them. This block-on-block continued until the resulting tower was perhaps waist high or until its wobble warned of a crash.

Then came the fun, six or seven peanuts, in the shell, were dropped, one at a time into the top of the tower. Each peanut would hurtle down through the lattice work and onto the floor at the base of the tower. What glorious fun! But wait, here was my invention, to make the breathtaking thrill of the drop even more outstanding, I laid one of our little iron fireman, from the hook and ladder, on his side at the bottom of the dropping tower and then pushed a block into the opening between the two foundation blocks, letting one end rest on the inert body of the fireman. This gave a pitch to the block and instead of the peanuts piling up in the base of the lattice tower they would hit the canted block and roll out onto the floor. Gee, that was clever!

Not one of these inventions, I reasoned, would give me the prestige that Tom had achieved. But they were a start, and besides I wasn't as old as Tom. Even the mechanical bell ringer which I rigged up one day using Mother's large pin cushion as a base was probably not patentable. A giant sized darning needle was pushed into the cushion, like a telegraph pole, my mother's gold thimble (the bell) was balanced on the needle, a little brass ring was tied to the end of a long thread and the thread was pushed through the eye of the darning needle. And so, by simply jiggling the thread, even from across the room, the ring would climb the needle, strike the thimble and make it tinkle. A glorious accomplishment.

Hardly worthy of mention, but I liked it – was the throttle lever which I constructed for my kerosene barrel locomotive. The barrel rested horizontally in a wooden cradle at the corner of the house, just outside the kitchen door. The remnants of a dilapidated orange crate served as the engineer's seat in the imaginary cab, close up behind the boiler (barrel) of my engine. A big mouthed jar containing a sloppy mud mixture sat on the deck to the right of my seat. A piece of wood lath was stuck in this mud and the upper end of this lath was well within my grasp. This was the throttle. When I pushed it forward, it resisted, sort of like a dashpot[51] because of the mud. Same resistance when I pulled it backwards. The mud for lever resistance was my very own invention, it gave somewhat of a measure of resistance to the throttle, and pleased me very much. Although I have since learned that the throttle lever on steam locomotives was mounted on top of the boiler and operated by the engineer's left hand. I loved it. B-o-y, wasn't I easily amused in those days.

---

[51] A mechanical device, a damper which resists motion by way of friction.

DO YOU HAVE A CRUCIAL NUMBER

I have! From the time when I was first able to toddle to the top of the stairway, turn, look down it's precipitous length and then casually topple off the top step and bump bump bump down other sixteen steps, ending upside down on the floor of the hallway, (I know that the number of steps totaled seventeen, not from my personal knowledge, not from counting the bumps as I went down, I couldn't count at that age, but because my big brother P.W. had told me there were seventeen.) No, seventeen is not my crucial number. I say from that time until the present I have been cautioned that it was bad luck to count the carriages in a funeral procession.

I waited until I was seven before succumbing to this challenge. But one day at Fourteenth and Liberty, probably on my devious way home from school, I encountered such a procession and wishing to take, what I considered a dare and tempt fate, I counted those carriages, not just once but twice. They totaled nine, including the pièce de résistance, the glass plated wagon which was responsible for the whole tour. You would conclude from the foregoing observation that my crucial number is nine. - Taint so! I have no idea for whom the bell tolled nor why the parade was venturing up Liberty Street past Fourteenth, but I did assume that he, or she had died.

And then there was the time when John Jeffery Louis and I were at 341 McGregor. We were both about thirteen at the time, John was justly proud of his family heritage and the way his surname was spelled, he was apparently related (through his father) to some saint in Missouri. On the occasion when I first met John he bet me that I was not familiar with the L-O-U-I-S spelling of his last name. It wasn't the common L-E-W-I-S with which so many people of that name are handicapped. I didn't take his bet, for Joe Louis, the fisticuffer[52] had not yet appeared

---

[52] One who fights with the fists.

on the scene and Louisville was just an undisclosed dream, besides Louie, the French king had a foreign surname.

John and I were sitting there at the old drop leaf desk in my bedroom, composing an order for magical supplies from Johnson, Smith Company in Chicago. We got to the end of the request with some difficulty, mainly due to the drippy, scratchy, dip-and-try pen. Then we came to the suffix and couldn't agree on whether to say "yours respectively" or "yours respectfully." We had reached a stalemate and finally decided to use "yours truly."

As we were affixing the pink Geo. Washington, two cent to the envelope of the finished document we heard the clanging bell of a police patrol, horse drawn of course, struggling up Reading Road towards McMillan Street. We rushed down stairs and took off in hot pursuit. We passed the patrol wagon within the next block while the team was being rested. That road was steep!

A sizeable crowd was gathered at the corner where the electric power plant for the street car system was located, right next door to the car barn. We learned from a talkative man in this assembly that one of the coal shovelers at the power house had gone across the street to rush the growler[53] and on his way back from the saloon he had stumbled in front of a fast moving street car going down the hill. His tin bucket of beer was thrown violently into the air and he was pretty well ground up under the car. Such are the vicissitudes of life.

---

[53] To take a container, usually a tin pail, to the local bar to buy beer.

'JEVER DAY DREAM

And then there was the time when I was riding on the big electric car on which I was making one of my very infrequent trips to Mineral Springs. The car stopped at a switch-back to allow the Franklin bound car to pass. We waited, perhaps five minutes, not more. I looked out the window at the calm Allegheny River flowing down towards Pittsburgh and the Ohio. There across the river I could see the shining rails of the Lehigh Valley's single track.

In the distance, down stream, appeared a locomotive, zipping along at high speed, pulling (what in those days) was a full string of box cars, ten, or possibly twelve with a tiny red caboose bringing up the rear. I was entranced by the sight of that little engine whirring along silently, because of the distance, with pistons pumping and driving rods flashing in the afternoon sunlight. The locomotive wheels weren't round, they were elliptical, bringing to my mind big brother P.W.'s many hasty sketches, in his school books, of fast moving locomotives.

What would I do if I was the last person in the world? No big ocean liner for me to play with at the steering wheel in the pilot house. No, not even the motorman's platform of a streetcar like the one on which I was now riding with no one to forbid me from seizing the controller and brake lever and taking off wherever the track would lead. I would choose the biggest and most elaborate locomotive which could be found and, like Casey Jones, mount to the cabin, find that Lehigh Valley stretch of track, down river from Franklin and open the throttle, gingerly at first to give me the feel of that great iron monster under my command, then wider and wider as we gained speed. I could hear the reverberating puffs of the exhaust and feel the side-to-side motion of the cab as I reached for the whistle cord and pulled it lustily.

Nor was I disturbed about the fact that if there was no fireman to shovel coal into the furnace, nor to keep watch on the water level in that great boiler, that this journey would not last for long. The thrill of my immediate pleasure was all that concerned me. But of course that was just a fantastic day dream.

In a mild way I had that dream partially fulfilled many years later when I became terminal superintendent at the then almost defunct refinery. It was necessary to keep up steam in the huge boiler house for pumps and fire fighting. To drag in the coal cars, pull out the cinder cars and spot the occasional tank cars which were loaded with lubricating oil, it was also necessary to keep our little steam yard locomotive on the active list. The plant night watchman tended the banked fire and at six o'clock in the morning he stoked the fire and raised steam for the day's work. As it would not be profitable to assign a regular engineer to handle this "yard boy" for intermittent and periodic shuffling of cars, I, on occasion would assume this engineman position myself, stoking the fire box, feeding water to the boiler through the old style steam injector and playing conductor, switchman, fireman and "best of all" engineer. Alone, no interference, on that one or two mile stretch of terminal service track.

Steam brakes replaced air brakes on this little "shuttlecock" but the polished brass brake lever, the throttle and the big reverse bar were exact duplicates of the ones on that enormous iron horse which I used to dream of.

The bell rope came into the cab on both the engineer's and the fireman's side. The whistle cord did not end, as I had pictured it, in a swinging wooden handle such as the old chain-pull toilets boasted, but rather with a cast-iron lever fastened to the roof of the cab directly over my head. The steam pressure gauge looked me directly in the face. The screen-protected water glass was visible from my perch below the right-hand cab window, the three little supplementary brass petcocks poked out of the boiler header at two inch intervals. These were for checking the accuracy of the water gauge the glass of which sometimes got clogged. A control chain hung loosely from the firebox door and jingled merrily when the engine was in motion.

Boy! How I loved these short interludes from my regular duties with pen or pencil or typewriter! Like a dream come true.

Oh if I'd only been twenty years younger at the time!

WHAT A DIFFERENCE 70-60-50 YEARS HAS MADE[54]
(In "Moom Pitchers," "Aireoplanes," And Wireless Telephony)

And then there was the time when I attended a gymnastic performance at the Franklin YMCA - I was about five years old and we, my Mom, Pop, P. W., Bert and myself were there. Interesting pleasures were few and far between in those days. I remember sitting on half of one of those horrible, collapsible chairs, (Bert had the other half) waiting to be entertained by Indian club and dumbbell drills etc. by the older boys when Robert Sweeney, a thirteen year old boy, stood up on the flying rings and proceeded to swing himself. At first he was greeted by a smattering of applause. As he swung higher and higher, more handclapping and a few shouts of acclaim were heard. The response of the spectators urged him to make an ultimate effort and he swung up almost to the overhanging balcony. Then Mr. Robinson, the Y secretary rushed out on the floor, shook a finger at the flying Robert and made him desist. Gee, I wished that I could swing on those rings!

After the callisthenic performance, which was dreary, Mr. Robinson announced that a Mr. Berland was going to show some magic lantern slides. They also were dreary, up to the final picture which was a cartoon of a very, very long eared donkey just standing there on white sheet background, suddenly he switched his tail and winked one eye. The applause for this antic was thunderous and the spectators all left in a jovial mood - thanks to the wonders of animation.

That must have been about the year 1898 - seventy years ago. "Gollies" how motion pictures have changed!

And then there was the time when Cliff Duttenhofer and his father took me, and maybe Bert, to a charity affair at Latonia, to see the much advertised Barney Oldfield and his "Green Dragon" speed around the track. An added feature was the appearance of two Glen Curtiss biplanes. Glen himself was going to pilot one of the planes. And not to

---

[54] GHSII wrote this in 1968.

160

be disregarded, was to be the performance of Roy Knabenshue with his lighter-than-air flying machine.

Knabenshue and his "flying cigar" were first to appear. He buzzed the grandstand with, what appeared to be, careless abandon, driving (flying) towards the crowd at high speed and at the last possible moment he would work himself back on the triangular frame and bring the nose of the machine up and away from the spectators. A practice which would not be tolerated today.

A few local automobile dealers raced their cars around the track individually, without competition. The purpose of this demonstration was either to show how fast their product would go, or perhaps to prove that it would run. The last of these "locals" to appear was the air cooled Franklin entry, which did not set the track on fire with it's speed but smoked profusely from the tail pipe and from under the hood.

Barney appeared next, sitting in his Peerless Green Dragon. He had a short stub of a cigar clamped solidly between his teeth. The mechanic, who stood in front of the "Dragon" to crank it's engine, beamed happily with a wide grin at Barney. Gosh! Again how much I envied that mechanic and his seeming friendship with the great Barney Oldfield. Finally, Barney took off and twice rounded the track at a fabulous rate of speed. The spectators cheered.

The airplanes had not flown yet but had been wheeled out, one behind the other onto the track. Magnificent kites of bamboo and canvas with a single engine and a wooden propeller (Pusher type) jutting out behind. There was some delay in getting the two planes to take off, they hadn't even started their engines. A man with a megaphone, announced that they were waiting for the wind to die down. Another man with a white handkerchief was standing near the planes, holding the handkerchief between his thumb and forefinger, apparently to test the velocity of the wind. The handkerchief hung limply, scarcely moving. The crown shouted, "Come on Glen, lets fly."

The megaphone man called out that while we were waiting for the wind to die, Mr. Ryan would drive his Sterns in a timed speed trial twice around the oval. Johnny Ryan, a local well known dare devil, brought his stripped Stearns out to the starting position, arranged for a friend to stand on the inside running board, hand onto the front seat and lean out as far as possible to keep the car from turning over. The speed of this trial run was phenomenal and the crowd shouted, "Bring out your Green Dragon, Johnny can best it!"

The management apparently was now convinced that the planes must fly. The both were started and circled the track once, in tandem – lifting off as much as ten feet into the air as they came to the grandstand.

That must have been about the year 1909 - sixty years ago. "Gollies," how airplanes have changed!

And then there was the time, during my Navy enlistment, when I was stationed in Cambridge, Massachusetts, when my buddy Arthur Williams had volunteered to go to New London, Connecticut to learn the ins and outs of radio telephony. After a few weeks at New London, he returned to Cambridge, filled with the wonders of this new branch of radio communication. He was filled with wonder and said to me, breathlessly, "Why Stan do you know that while I was testing a set on a destroyer at the dock down there, I distinctly heard the voice of Radio Chief Felton, whom I know quite well. He was on a destroyer stationed off Block Island, that's thirty five miles away from New London." I asked him what Chief Felton had said, Art replied, "Why Stan he said just as plain, 'hello there'."

That was in the year 1918 – Just fifty years ago. - Oh well!

EXCERPTS FROM LETTERS

LETTER TO PAUL WOOD STANSBURY[55] 9/12/1964

. . . An item "nostalgic" presents itself, even though you have intimated that you are not interested in looking back. Personally I enjoy the practice and am convinced that I remember happenings in the past much more vividly than those which have not yet taken place, i.e. the future, I say the future if there is any such thing.

THE INCIDENT - One quiet evening (some time ago) big brother P.W. was seated comfortably in the old wicker chair in the kitchen of number 12, Sixteenth Street. Why you were in the kitchen, I don't remember; perhaps it was because that cozy old chair, a Maggie DeWoody symbol was there first. Callow George was there too and he was sleepy but inspired. He would compose a book of music. Perhaps he was six, possibly seven. At any rate in the Alice Brady first grade, he had mastered the art of printing his own name. The inspiration was partly due to the little pocket note book which he had, tightly clutched, in his grubby little hand. The book contained, in addition to a calendar, about twenty lined blank pages. The front cover of this tiny book was a brilliant red and bore in gold letters the word NOTES, followed by, in larger print, CHARLES HARRIS – FINE SHOES. No Franklin Pa., no Thirteenth Street. But why should it? – everybody knew that department store – the epitome of commercial activity.

Oh well, as I said you were at leisure and George was sleepy yet inspired. He "headed up" the book and began composing. I enclose, for your edification and wastebasket, a facsimile (from Memory) of this three page masterpiece. George did the first page himself and then worried brother P.W. into completing the symphony, beginning on page two and bursting into a cymbal-crashing finale on page three.

Several months later I retrieved the little red book from its hiding place beneath the slaw grater in the kitchen double drawer and with the

---

[55] Referred to in the correspondence as P.W.

valued help of brother Bert I read the George Stansbury music book in its entirety, all three pages . . .

LETTER TO PAUL WOOD STANSBURY – 12/1965

... Have heard of Fly and Frank, but Mose Kerr is the only Mose that I recall. But since you initiated the subject (or did you?) how about Arch, Newton, Harold and Gilbert? All Osmers of course and "Old Lady" Osmer who, by candle light, was prone to sit in her parlor at night and beat on the piano with unmerciful gusto. The departed spirits were able to translate those loud discords into soft heavenly music. And then there was Eph, the pipe-smoking Osmer handyman, Douglas, never appreciated to Doug, the black house boy in the David McCalmont service. He, rumor has it, was required to sweep the rugs with a whisk broom. Long handled broom stirred up too much dust.

Mr. Butcher, whom I envied because it was understood that he earned one dollar a day as a ditch digger. Mrs. "Hoity Toity" Wernicke who never appeared outside of her own domicile. In that hospital lacking little oil town there also were two foot power (by necessity) dentists, Drs. Turley and Richards, neither of whom gave a damn about straightening my front uppers. As a consequence they are still crooked, the teeth, not the oral jacklegs. In this connection, I note in the book Magic, Myth and Medicine (which you so thoughtfully donated to the cause) that dentists in many states were not required, until the year 1900, to obtain a license in order to pursue the practice of dentistry. Gad aren't we lucky to be alive!

I give up on St. Clair's custom tailor uncle. I did know an Uncle Eddie of that clan, a practical carpenter who carried a cloth sack of fine cut tobacco in his hip pocket and slowed down production by seeking it out and replenishing his cud, (I hate the word) between hatchet blows. I was so enthralled with Uncle Eddie's fine cut habit while he was rebuilding the Riesenman back porch and I was overseeing the work that I prevailed upon my mother to buy me a package of Baker's shredded cocoanut and to construct, for my use, a little cloth bag similar to a Bull Durham package. This I filled with shredded cocoanut and proudly carried it in my jumper pocket – my trousers didn't boast a hip

167

pocket – I strutted, chewed cocoanut and emulated that slow moving carpenter until my supply of cocoanut was exhausted. And that's all I know about the Riesenman custom tailor. Possibly he and Uncle Eddie were the same person. For about a year later when that back porch collapsed, I concluded that Uncle Eddie was no carpenter.

Well practically all of this one sided discussion dates back to the nineteenth century, but you mentioned Booth of the 1800's and even big George who began operations in 1732. Yep it's a long drag from Caesar's sharpened clam shell to the present stainless steel blades. Remember, my Pop[56] (and yours) for many years wouldn't switch from his straight razor to a safety because he maintained that King C. Gillette, whose likeness appeared on early blade wrappers, looked like a charlatan . . .

---

[56] George Herbert Stansbury Sr.

LETTER TO PAUL WOOD STANSBURY – 4/1966

. . . Here enters an opportunity to thank you for saving my life, a belated thank you, but at the time of the saving I was only about one and one half years old[57] and at that tender age I could scarcely comprehend what you had done (or attempted to do) for me. In recent years I have reminded myself of the incident and will attempt to relate it, assuming that it has completely slipped from your memory.

The low level, pantry junk drawer contained a great many fabulous trinkets, Jim-cracks[58] and artifacts of tremendous interest to a very small boy. Someone had carelessly left this drawer partially open and I toddled into the pantry, plopped down on the floor and began a piece by piece inspection of these long forbidden treasures. There were wheels from an abandoned cast iron fire engine held together by a wire axle, nails of various sizes, corks, empty medicine bottles, a tack hammer with a tack puller attached in place of the claw, a hammer (by the way) to which Carl Read referred as the "rattle" because the tack pulling jaw was loosely riveted to the head and when a tack was driven with it a sound much like a baby rattle was apparent.

But I'm not eulogizing the tack hammer, I'm concerned with a piece of bluestone (copper sulphate) some of which my Pop used to energize the wet cells which provided electric power for the front door bell. This find was a beautiful blue crystal about the size of a hulled black walnut. It was almost transparent and undoubtedly good to eat.

I tasted it cautiously. It was disappointingly bitter and I removed it from my mouth and sat there contemplating it critically, clenching it tightly in my, now slobbery, hand. This examination was proceeding to my liking when my mother appeared on the scene, snatched me from the floor, poked her finger into my cavernous mouth to retrieve any particles of the gem which I had not swallowed. Her finger and my tongue an lips were all tinged a beautifully delicate pastel blue. I

---

[57] Circa 1894.
[58] Most likely 'gimcracks': cheap and showy ornaments; knickknacks.

screamed, not because of the poison which I had not eaten, but from being deprived of those red fire engine wheels which I had been clutching in my left fist and was forced to relinquish when I was so unceremoniously snatched from the floor.

My mother looked at my blue lips and was completely horrified. She immediately dispatched you, on the run, to summon Dr. Wallace from his office. That big box telephone on the wall never entered her distraught mind. Or perhaps it was my incessant squalling which made her realize than an uninterrupted conversation by phone was impossible.

You zipped out of the house at top speed, turned the corner from Sixteenth Street into Elk Street on two wheels and dashed pell mell towards the Doctor's office. As the story was told to me, your father, on his way home from work, was just bidding Ed Grimm good bye in front of "Grimmie's" house when you hove into sight, but still travelling at top speed. He attempted to intercept you but you had been assigned a mission and were determined to carry it to a proper conclusion, come hell, high water or an inquiring father.

The outcome of this adventure has never been told to me. Was the Doctor at home? Did he come to my (my mother's) rescue? Suffice it is to say that my big brother's determination to outwit catastrophe and give his all (at least a temporary delay in his perusal of an interesting chapter of the Gollywog Book) for the sake of a stupid little runny-nosed brother was successful. And if further proof of the efficacy of your jaunt is required – my present address is 5801 Stansbury Lane, and I am still kicking. I herewith confer on you an A for effort . . .

LETTER TO PAUL WOOD STANSBURY – 9/1966

. . . Concerning the enclosed "Cider Lady" story. You are the only remaining member of the "succor party" to be classed among the quick. Fact is, although I don't know the current status of John and Georgie Berlin, I'll bet a whole bag of marbles against a "keyster" that your two brothers are the only survivors of the original, venturesome exploration group. Say, all three of those Sternberg[59] boys have already out-aged their Pop. You say that's not so remarkable. But a happy thought anyway . . .

---

[59] Referring to the presumed name of the family when they emigrated to America.

LETTER TO PAUL WOOD STANSBURY – ?

. . . You mention that frightening sound of the F.F.D[60] bell. I thought that the ominous sound of that bell was a "born in" idiosyncrasy with me alone and I have hesitated to mention it. It scared me too, especially after dark. Say - now that you have broken the ice, another fearful sound that I remember from my early youth was the mournful wail of the alarm whistle on a "gathering" tank at the Galena refinery. I didn't know it at the time of my first exposure to it, but, as I found out in later life it was an automatic warning whistle which blew when a processing tank which had almost reached it's capacity, was in danger of overflowing. Gad, that low moan echoing across French Creek made my flesh creep.

I remember one evening Bobby Read and I were walking up Sixteenth Street. and had reached the flag pole in front of Mom Bridge's house when that eerie whistle sounded. I asked Bobby what it meant and he whispered to me "Bear's paw lost." He had no more idea of the source or the cause of that sound than I did. But Bobby was imaginative and simply said the first nonsensical thing that entered his mind. For days, even years, I had visions of a rejected bear's paw, leg and all, wandering aimlessly through the Franklin hills searching for his parents. Gosh, I must have been a stupid little brat and scared too . . .

---

[60] Franklin Fire Department

172

LETTER TO PAUL WOOD STANSBURY – 10/1968

. . . Speaking of Harry Kellar, as I am about to do, do you remember taking your two little brothers to see him – I think it was the Grand Theater in Cincinnati? We arrived early and were comfortably seated in the third or fourth row. A disturbance a few rows in back of us attracted our attention. Several ushers and the manager were attempting to convince an elderly and rather portly woman that she was not entitled to the seat which she was then occupying. You assured Bert and me that the woman had a standing room ticket with which she was threatening the manager. The orchestra sounded off with "Honey Boy" and we lost interest in the fight . . .

. . . So that was the Allegheny Valley R.R. – stupid little me. What I can best recall of the Franklin railroads were the three stations, Erie, LS&MS[61] and Valley. The Erie was across the creek, the Valley was across the river and the LS&MS was down town and handy. Of course your "little brother" didn't have all of your railroading advantages, such as your first paying job, which was, I recall, clerk in the Cin'ti. CH & D office[62]

Do I remember correctly? Sometimes when a three or four car passenger train was coming into the station, I saw the conductor and the brakeman on the car platforms twisting the brake wheels to keep the little coffeepot locomotive from overshooting it's mark, as it rounded the Buffalo Street bend. Right? Wrong? – What no air brakes? Talked to CBS[63] a few days ago and even he, master historian that he is, didn't question my observation that the Lehigh Valley R.R. ran around the edge of Franklin via the far shore of the Allegheny River. Live and learn say I.

Frequently, when an LS&MS freight pulled through Fourteenth Street, our Pop would stand on the sidewalk at the top of Liberty Street at Sixteenth. And when the poor little overburdened engine slipped it's drivers[64] attempting to drag those cars around the curves at both ends of Fourteenth Street, our Pop would call out, aiming at the engineer, who was of course much too far off to hear him, "give her sand Eddie, give her sand." Ella Bridge would appear on "Mom" Bridges front porch and stare in amazement at our Pop, and then shake her head and disappear into the house . . .

---

[61] Lake Shore and Michigan Southern Railway (1869-1914)
[62] Cincinnati, Hamilton and Dayton Railway (1846–1917)
[63] Charles Bertram Stansbury, a brother.
[64] Drive wheels

LETTER TO PAUL WOOD STANSBURY – 2/1969

. . . You say that you can't recall what cousin Lee was delivering in his bread wagon. Oh, I can answer that one and I'll try to do so in a future "And then there was the time" item. – And he snapped his whip at the feasting sparrows by the road side! Do you recall the 38 caliber, 5 shot, hair trigger (without a guard) nickel plated revolver that our Pop used to maintain in the second from the top chiffonier drawer at twelve Sixteenth Street? On questioning our mother as to why and what for he had it, she asserted that Herb used it to shoot robins, apparently to help supply the family larder and add variety to the festive board. If he could hit a robin with that nickel plated hazard, he must sure have shot over his shoulder in the dead of night while sighting his quarry with a mirror held in his teeth. Must'a been pure luck, I mean.

Them there wheel twisting conductors and brakemen were definitely seen by yours truly on the LS&MS from a vantage point at the top of Liberty street hill, on the sidewalk of Sixteenth Street between the Strausburg and Dan Bridge homesteads. How in the world could I have seen across French Creek to the Erie R.R. from such a place as that? This braking was not a daily occurrence, but only occasionally, understand, that's why I inquired, "What, no air brakes?" . . .

LETTER TO PAUL WOOD STANSBURY – 1969

. . . Do you remember the bottle of "schnapps"[65] that our Pop used to keep in the "master" bedroom at 12 Sixteenth Street? That bottle probably lasted from about 1895 through 1903 and the Bourbon hadn't receded from the neck of the bottle in all that time. 'Twas only used medicinally of course, a few (I mean few) drops on a lump of sugar from the wooden hamper which was stored in the "under the attic stairway closet" in your bedroom, for sore throat, toothache or a sprained head. That wooden sugar hamper, as I remember it was barrel sized – but I'll bet that little bucket didn't hold more than two quarts.

Same thing is true of that old red chest of drawers in that same bedroom. The bottom drawer was a junk drawer for Bert's and my exclusive use. The third drawer from the bottom was yours, where among other treasures, you kept the cotton padded and partitioned cigar box of pretty, blown birds eggs. That's the same chest which had seven drawers in it, but my big brother P.W. maintained there were eight and proved it to me by counting from the top, pointing to each drawer as he called out it's number. Somewhere between three and four he would pull a "switcheroo" on me and add one drawer to the total.

I always came away from that counting ordeal, alone, mystified and helpless. Sneaking back into the room by myself, I would count and recount those drawers always arriving at my original figure of seven. Chee! How gullible I must have been . . .

---

[65] The generic term for all white (clear) brandies.

. . . And speaking of fire departments, do you recall, in Cin'ti days, the six foot long four by four timber, painted red, with an iron fitting on the end and a rubber bumper on the other, carried by most steam pumpers (horse drawn of course) for the purpose of letting a streetcar assist the horses by pushing the engine up a steep grade? The fireman driver just arranged to stay on the car tracks and eventually a streetcar would come clanging along.

The water-tender on the pumper would attach the iron fitting of the four by four to the front coupler of the car and then, cautiously guide the rubber bumper end to fit on the back step of his machine. Then, much to the astonishment of the horses, the whole cavalcade would hasten up the hill.

I recall such a procession meandering up Reading Road past McGregor Ave. - the two white horses, stepping high and holding their heads at "look-a-me" level. Our Pop remarked from the front porch, "Just look at those horses, they imagine they have suddenly become as strong as atlas." . . .

. . . Speaking of fire departments and our Pop's disdain for Cin'ti. in general.

Do you remember how he used to read an account of a fire in the paper? The Times-Star would invariably end the story with - "Marshal-on-the-spot then turned in the ten-blow.[66] With what disgust Pop would sneer at the words, "Marshal-on-the-spot," and with what a burst of pent up animosity and even anger he would slur the reporter's words, "Then turned in the ten-blow." Brother, did he show his temper! I have never been informed of why he disapproved of either "Marshal" or "Ten-blow" - but he apparently knew . . .

. . . Mother was conversing with Anna Myers on our big wall phone. I of course, knew that my father spent his working hours in that little polished box under the "speaker-snout" of the instrument, but I couldn't figure how there was room in there for Anna too. Asked Mother to let me hear her. She pulled up a chair for me to stand on, held the receiver to my ear and told me to begin the conversation, aiming my mouth at the afore mentioned "speak-snout." I finally overcame my timidity to the point where I hesitatingly said "Lo." – Anna's voice came back through the receiver, "Why hello, who is this?" Then wonder of wonders, I replied in clear, mellow tones, presaging the magnificent mind of my future development, "It's me." Since that first phone conversation some 74 years ago,[67] I have never liked to give, or receive messages by way of the telephone – they seem so stilted . . .

---

[66] The editor surmises this refers to delivering a knock out blow. The boxer is knocked down and is unable to continue the fight within a ten-second count. In this instance the fire was dealt a knock out blow.

[67] Circa 1896.

LETTER TO PAUL WOOD STANSBURY – 4/7/1970

. . . I have a vivid picture of Liberty Street on an afternoon (many years ago) when the snow was deep but bobsleds were functioning. Four or five boys were assembled in the street in front of Grant's house - busily rolling immense snowballs and escorting them out to the speedway in the center of the street, and then, when a sled loaded with men, (boys) impelled by the first one hundred yards of that steep hill - too late to stop - too precarious to steer around those enormous balls of snow, the sled would smack directly into them.

Then the hold-up team (bombing crew) would close in and pelt the distraught and almost defenseless sledders with snow balls of conventional size. Don't remember just who made up that derailing crew - probably Harry and Red Grant along with many others, one of whom was my big brother P.W. who was active in both rolling and placing the "bombs" in the freeway and firing the snowballs at those interrupted and hostile travelers. I watched the battles from the vantage point of our front porch. I recognized you because of your red stocking cap bobbing and sashaying up and down as you joined the others in your hellish attempts to interfere with those helpless passengers on the bobsleds . . .

. . . Nearly Easter now – which brings on a feeling of nostalgia for the old Franklin days. For instance, do you remember that Easter morning when, at P.W.'s call, you and I rushed into his room? He was lying on his back in bed. Over his head, dancing mysteriously, was a strange little egg shaped man.

I don't know how it affected you, but to me the mystery this dancing egg (I finally realized that it was an egg) cavorting in mid air with no visible means of support, above my brother's head, was something from out of this world.

Amazed as I was, I stood there staring at this phenomenon for perhaps a full minute before in the half light of the early morning I got a glimpse of the black supporting thread.

P.W. had ingeniously tied a thread between the head and foot of his iron bed, had blown the works out of a chicken egg to make it lighter, painted a ludicrous face on the shell and suspended it from the "head-to-foot" thread – and by merely pushing his feet against the upright bars of the bed, caused the egg to dance in a most puzzling manner above his upturned face.

Gosh, wasn't I susceptible to delusions? You two brothers had chosen what might be called a rather stupid third brother . . .

EPILOGUE

FINDING GEORGE

On Easter Day, 2016, James, John and Paul Stansbury began planning a pilgrimage to Franklin, Pennsylvania to visit the birthplace of their Grandfather, George Herbert Stansbury, Jr. (GHS).

They had 3 objectives in mind: 1) find the house where he lived, 2) find and identify as many of the houses, businesses and places mentioned in his reminiscences as possible, and 3) enjoy the experience and each other's company.

In May of 2016, they arrived in Franklin, checking into a B&B on Fifteenth Street just down the Liberty Street hill from where they believed GHS's house to be. They were sure that one of two houses at the top of Liberty Street, where it ended at Sixteenth Street, had to be the Stansbury House. They hoped an appointment with the Venango County Historical Society the following day would reveal which it was.

At the historical society, they examined various documents including property records. *The New Atlas of the City of Franklin* published in 1915 was particularly helpful. From one of GHS's stories, they knew the house had been sold to the Huntington family. The atlas contained a plat which showed the location of the house owned in 1915 by Kate M. Huntington on Sixteenth Street. Having solved the riddle of the house, they visited St. John's Episcopal Church where they had the good fortune to find records of the baptisms of Paul Wood, Charles Bertram and George Herbert Jr. That afternoon, they returned to Sixteenth Street to stand proudly in front of their Grandfather's boyhood home.

Before leaving Franklin, they enjoyed a special meal at a special place: The Commons At Franklin. At the turn of the 20th Century, it was known as The Nursery Club. In another of his stories, GHS described sitting on its steps. They could not pass up the opportunity to sit on those steps, just as their Grandfather had done as a boy 116 years earlier. At the end of their meal, they participated in a final tribute to their Grandfather, sharing a Cammamaler Cake.

They left Franklin, satisfied that they had met their objectives. However, one of them had yet one more discovery to share:

In December of 2016, at a Christmas family gathering, John Stansbury presented James and Paul each with a special present along with the following explanation:

In May of 2016, the three amigos took a trip to Franklin, PA, the birthplace of our grandfather. We went to take pictures of the homestead and to see if it was possible to recover the special childhood treasure of our grandfather, Carbon Electrodes. While taking pictures of the house we spoke to Mrs. Kassi the owner of the house. We did not say anything to her about the treasure because the area under the porch looked inaccessible. We were in town for several days so one day when Jim and Paul were taking their naps, I gained enough courage to go back to the house to try to see if I could get the owners to let me check out Grandfathers tale of his treasure. Dr. and Mrs. Kassi were very interested in the story. They said they had bought the house in November of 2014 and had never been under the porch, but they granted me permission to enter a side opening under the porch and begin my quest for Grandfather's treasure. I used my cell phone flashlight and searched along the floor joist and the brick pillars that supported the joist. I was under the porch for about 30 to 40 minutes watching out constantly for any critters. I finally discovered up on one of the center pillars next to a floor joist grandfathers treasure. There were 2 intact carbon electrodes and a slightly broken or used electrode. Jim and Paul have the 2 intact electrodes and I kept the used one.

John Stansbury

Sheppard Press